SPRINGFIELD
Between Two Rivers

An Illustrated History

By Dorothy Velasco and Mara Velasco
Profiles by Pete Malliris and Kim Sullivan
Produced in cooperation with the
Springfield Area Chamber of Commerce

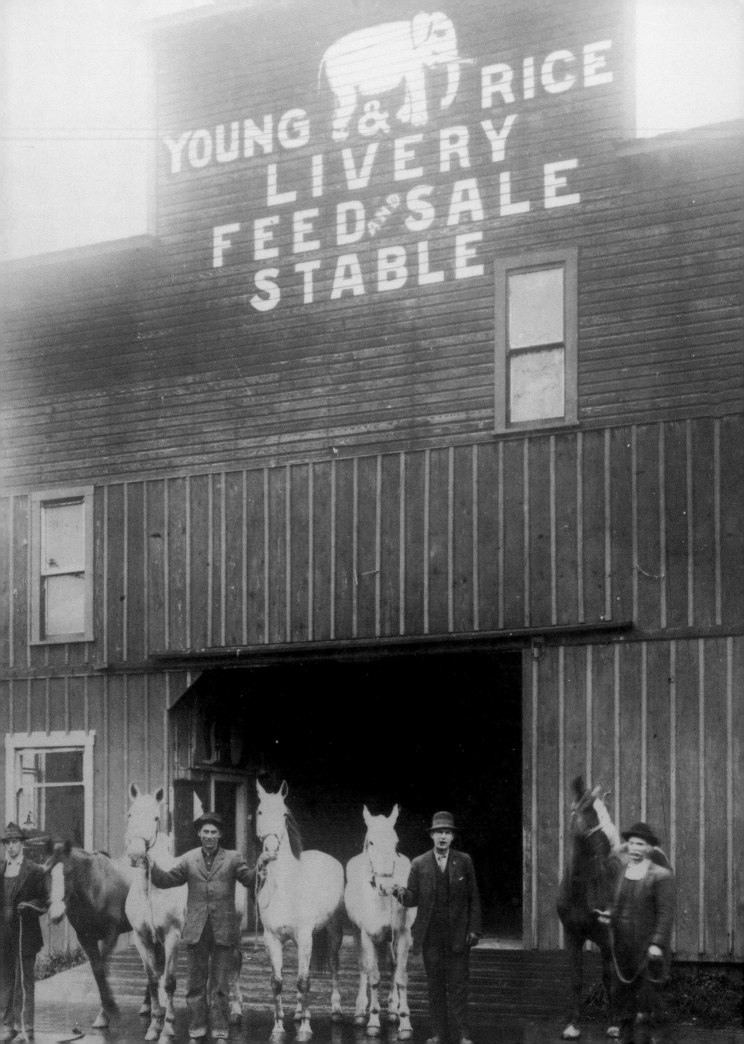

SPRINGFIELD
Between Two Rivers

An Illustrated History

Springfield: Between Two Rivers
An Illustrated History
By: DOROTHY VELASCO AND MARA VELASCO
Corporate Profiles by: PETE MALLIRIS AND KIM SULLIVAN

Community Communications, Inc.
Publishers: RONALD P. BEERS AND JAMES E. TURNER

Staff for *Between Two Rivers: An Illustrated History of Springfield*
Publisher's Sales Associate: MARLENE BERG
Executive Editor: JAMES E. TURNER
Senior Editor: MARY SHAW HUGHES
Managing Editor: KURT R. NILAND
Profile Editors: KARI COLLIN JARNOT AND MARY CATHERINE RICHARDSON
Editorial Assistant: AMANDA J. BURBANK
Design Director: SCOTT PHILLIPS
Designers: CHRIS ELLIOTT AND HOLLI T. HAWSEY
Photo Editors: KURT R. NILAND, CHRIS ELLIOTT AND HOLLI T. HAWSEY
Production Manager: JARROD STIFF
Contract Manager: CHRISTI STEVENS
National Sales Manager: JOHN HECKER
Sales Assistant: ANNETTE R. LOZIER
Proofreader: KARI COLLIN JARNOT
Accounting Services: SARA ANN TURNER
Printing Production: GARY G. PULLIAM/DC GRAPHICS
Pre-press & separations: ARTCRAFT GRAPHIC PRODUCTIONS

Community Communications, Inc.
Montgomery, Alabama

James E. Turner, Chairman of the Board
Ronald P. Beers, President
Daniel S. Chambliss, Vice President

The Young & Rice Livery Stable was still a thriving business in 1906, but the automobile was starting to change the way people traveled. Photo courtesy of the Springfield Museum.

Table of Contents

Photo courtesy of the Springfield Museum

Photo courtesy of the Springfield Museum

Foreword

Of all the populated places named "Springfield," there are thirty-six in the United States of America alone, and some states even have more than one Springfield! But what makes Springfield, Oregon so special? Why should there be a book about its history?

No doubt all the other Springfields have natural assets, perhaps even a spring in a field, but no other Springfield is nestled at the juncture of the Willamette and world-famous McKenzie Rivers. Other Springfields can even lay claim to some very famous people. But the people of Springfield, Oregon have consistently chosen to rise above circumstances and setbacks to persevere, and to succeed.

This combination of natural beauty and human spirit is worthy of a written history, and the Springfield Area Chamber of Commerce is very pleased to have been the catalyst to see that the story of Springfield is published. The idea of a history of Springfield had been floating around between various organizations and public officials for several years, but the chamber appeared to be in a unique position to gather sufficient support and sustain the effort. The chamber initiated this project as part of the celebration of its 50th anniversary, and the result is a delightfully readable and informative work that speaks to the loveliness of Springfield's surroundings and to the resiliency of its people.

This history book has a dimension not usually found in such efforts. As a tip of the hat to our numerous and generous underwriting sponsors, we have included their histories as well. These histories are gathered in a special section following the history of the city itself, and they are important to read. The history of Springfield is not complete without knowing about some of the successful businesses and organizations that have contributed to our community over the years.

Many of our sponsoring businesses are in their third or fourth generation of family ownership and management, which mirrors a lot of what is so great about Springfield. As citizens over the last one hundred plus years, we have chosen to learn from our past in order to prepare for our future as we continue to build for Springfielders yet to come. With this book we have a common reference. On behalf of the Springfield Area Chamber of Commerce, I invite you to read, learn, and enjoy!

Thomas E. Draggoo
Vice President, Centennial Bank
President, Springfield Area Chamber of Commerce

In the early part of the century, the streetcar between Springfield and Eugene was busiest on Saturdays, when shoppers and excursionists were out in force. Photo courtesy of the Springfield Museum.

Preface

Springfields exist throughout the United States. Many were named for older Springfields in the East. Springfield, Oregon, however, was named not for a former hometown but for an actual spring in a field. Elias and Mary Briggs, instead of memorializing their own names as founders, simply and pragmatically chose to describe their homestead.

These plain, unpretentious but enterprising pioneers were typical of the generations of hard workers that followed them. As soon as the early settlers could dig a millrace and build first a flour mill and then lumber mills, Springfield became a mill town. Now, 150 years later, it is no longer exclusively a mill town, but the remaining mills are still significant employers, and more importantly, still important icons imbedded in the psyche of a good many residents. Springfield High School's team name is the Millers, and no one has to ask what "Millers" stands for.

As you read this book you'll learn the history of Oregon's Springfield. In the spirit of civic improvement and community enhancement, Springfield's residents have cooperated in many endeavors, and argued about others. One topic we will never argue about is our love of Springfield's natural setting. In addition to the riches of the Willamette Valley, we are blessed to have designated tracts of wilderness nearby. Loggers and environmentalists, developers and historic preservationists, children and grandparents, and immigrants and pioneer descendants all love the natural beauty that surrounds us.

We live close to the land in Springfield. We can step outside our doors and enjoy sparkling rivers, hills covered with Douglas fir, and every shade of green visible to humans. In an hour or so we can drive to the mountains or the ocean. Springfield, Oregon, surely has the most beautiful setting of any Springfield in the country. We have been blessed.

Dorothy Velasco
Mara Velasco

The Deadmond Ferry transported people across the McKenzie to the Seavey Hops Yard. Smith Mountjoy photo courtesy of the Springfield Museum.

THE FIRST
SPRINGFIELDERS

When the first white people laid eyes upon the
Willamette Valley in western Oregon, they found a land that
pleased them greatly. Only sparsely populated by Native peoples,
the grassy valley looked almost like a vast wheat field bisected
by crystal-clear rivers, marshes, and small lakes.

(above) An early explorer drew a Kalapuya hunter wearing a woven hat and skins. Drawing courtesy of the
University of Oregon Museum of Natural History. (right) The Kalapuya Indians lived in the Springfield area before
the pioneers arrived. Drawing by Patrick Curtis courtesy of the University of Oregon Museum of Natural History.

Vegetation seemed to appear overnight and grew with surprising speed. Large oaks covered the foothills. In what came to be known as the Cascade Mountains to the east and the Coast Range to the west, ancient conifers grew to unimaginable heights.

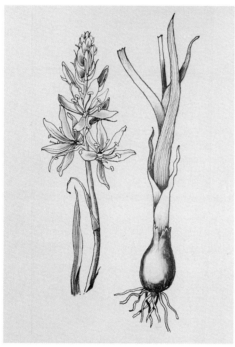

(above) The camas bears an iris-like blue flower. Its bulbous root was a food staple of the Kalapuyas, who protected its growing areas. They roasted the roots in underground pit ovens lined with rocks. The Kalapuyas also cultivated small patches of tobacco. Drawings by Patrick Curtis courtesy of the University of Oregon Museum of Natural History.

(right) Kalapuyas may have caught eels by hand in the area's rivers. Drawing by Patrick Curtis courtesy of the University of Oregon Museum of Natural History.

The first white people thought they were viewing a pristine wilderness, a land unchanged since creation. They didn't know they were seeing plant life manipulated by the hands of the Kalapuya Indians. They also didn't realize they were seeing the remains of a once-thriving culture.

If those explorers could have gone back in time 1000 years or more, they would have found numerous groups of inhabitants speaking related dialects. Three Kalapuyan languages formed the Kalapuyan Family of the Penutian stock of languages.

Kalapuyas lived in small villages containing extended families, generally a patriarch and his descendants. Groups of closely related villages formed bands sharing a designated territory. Wives usually came from other villages and joined their husbands' families.

For thousands of years plants provided the staples for Kalapuya bands inhabiting the valley, and game, water fowl, and fish abounded. The Kalapuya were not among the wealthiest of Oregon tribes, but they lived in a degree of comfort and stability.

Their primary food source, and an important trade item, was the bulb of the camas, or wild blue lily. Somewhat similar to small onions, the bulbs could be eaten raw in late spring. By June huge camas harvests commenced each year and continued throughout the summer. Kalapuyas dug the bulbs with a sharp yew stick and slowly cooked them in rock-lined pit ovens, transforming the bulbs' starches into digestible sugars. They then dried the bulbs and pounded them into cakes for winter storage or trade in the Columbia basin.

Another important food harvested in late summer was tarweed seed. This staple, similar to sunflower seed, was important enough that individual villages owned certain tarweed patches by common agreement. Kalapuyas gathered seeds by setting fire to the prairie plants, then beating the seeds from the stalks into baskets. They

Two beautiful rivers, the Willamette and the McKenzie, merge just northwest of Springfield. Photo courtesy of Springfield Chamber of Commerce.

parched the seeds, ground them into flour, and sometimes mixed them with mashed cooked camas and wild hazelnuts. Because the annual fires inhibited unwanted growth and encouraged the growth of even-age stands of plants, the valley took on the appearance of cultivated fields.

A fortuitous by-product of the field burning was the roasting of grasshoppers, a great delicacy. Another favorite treat was a type of caterpillar, roasted or boiled. It was easier, however, to fill a stomach with large game. Men hunted deer, elk, and black bear with spears or bow and arrows. Many birds and small mammals, as well as fish, eels, and crawfish, offered variety. Fish could be dried for the winter, and it was easy to obtain dried salmon from the Columbia River through trade.

The Kalapuya calendar, broadly divided into summer and winter, determined quite different living conditions

during each half of the year. During the growing season, which was relatively dry, people traveled to familiar food-gathering areas. They lived in temporary shelters of bark and branches and wore little clothing.

During the rainy half of the year, when dark clouds hid the hilltops and drenching was constant, Kalapuyas returned to their winter villages, living in low plank houses about 60 feet long and partly underground. Often multiple families shared the same house, which was divided into family compartments; the more families, the longer the house. A hole cut in the roof allowed smoke to exit.

In the winter both men and women put on warm elk-hide leggings and moccasins. Men wore buckskin shirts and trousers and women wore buckskin dresses. Both used cloaks and hats. As in most societies, prominent or wealthy people ornamented their attire with items of value, in this case dentalium shells (also known as tooth shells), porcupine quills, beads, and feathers. Nose and ear ornaments, necklaces, bracelets, and tattooing completed the adornments. Some Kalapuyas flattened their babies' heads with boards for additional refinement.

Chieftainship was passed in different ways, but invariably it involved wealth. In some cases the position was held by women. A few chiefs and other comparatively wealthy people occasionally owned slaves, generally captives acquired through trade. Kalapuyas were not active slave traders, however, and they were more likely the victims of slave raiders.

Long before white people first set foot in the Willamette Valley, their diseases preceded them. Ship traders stopped along the Oregon coast during the 1700s. Whenever sailors stepped ashore, they left a legacy of smallpox, malaria, venereal disease, and other deadly illnesses. In 1782-83 a smallpox epidemic swept through the Northwest. By the time Lewis and Clark arrived in 1805, they found a population already weakened by white man's diseases.

The first known contact between Whites and Kalapuyas occurred in 1812, when Donald McKenzie and a party of Pacific Fur Company traders explored the Willamette Valley. From that time until the coming of the homesteaders in the 1840s, Kalapuyas engaged in frequent trading with fur traders. In the 1830s Methodists established a mission in what would become the Salem area, but Kalapuyas had little contact with them.

From 1830-33 a malaria epidemic decimated the Kalapuya population, reducing it from an estimated 10,000 to approximately 350. When the first homesteaders arrived in the future Springfield area, they saw very few Kalapuya people, who evidently didn't bother them.

In 1846 pioneer leader Jesse Applegate, along with a handful of friends, forged a rough cutoff from the California Trail, veering up through southern Oregon to the Willamette Valley. Although the road, known then as the Southern Route and today as the Applegate Trail, effectively shortened the route to the southern and central Willamette Valley, the first travelers who risked it suffered enormous loss of life and property.

By 1848, however, the trail was better established, and increasing numbers traveled it safely. It was along this route that a young couple from Kentucky came seeking prosperity. They were soon to found the settlement they eventually called Springfield. ❶

Kalapuya homes, low structures of cedar logs and shakes, may have looked something like this model. Photo courtesy of The Springfield News.

(next page) The cold clear water of the McKenzie River teemed with fish and attracted countless waterfowl. Photo courtesy of the Springfield Museum.

Chapter Two

THE HOMESTEADERS
1849-1875

Like so many Americans in the mid-19th century, Elias and Mary Briggs could not resist the lure of the West. In 1848, the young couple packed their bags and began the long and arduous journey from their home in Kentucky to the Pacific Northwest. Traveling along the Southern Route, over the Cascade mountain range, and through the Rogue River Valley, the Briggses finally arrived in the sparsely populated Willamette Valley, just in time for a wet winter.

Elias Briggs as a mature man. The drawing was probably made from a photo. Courtesy of the Springfield Museum.

In October 1849, Elias took advantage of the Oregon Land Grant Program to acquire a 640-acre land claim on the east bank of the Willamette River. His claim, which lay between two buttes now known as Springfield Butte and Kelly Butte, included a low flat land graced with a bubbling spring. He built his cabin in that field and named the property Springfield, giving the future town a name.

Elias Briggs went on to do much more for Springfield than simply name it. Like Eugene Skinner who had recently settled a few miles away on the west bank of the Willamette, Briggs was a natural entrepreneur who set out to build a town. Although the California Gold Rush drew many pioneers away from the Northwest in the late 1840s, the efforts of Elias and a handful of community leaders ensured that Springfield grew slowly but surely.

Briggs' first venture (and the first recorded business in Springfield) was a ferry service across the Willamette River. Accounts of who founded the ferry business conflict: some say that William M. Stevens, a homesteader north of Springfield, founded the service in 1847 and later hired Briggs to run the business. Others tell just the opposite: Briggs created the business in 1849 and hired Stevens as manager. In any case, the river crossing came to be known as the "Briggs Ferry," and it provided a much-needed service, particularly for those hurrying south to the California gold fields. Crossing the river was no easy matter in the 1840s. Wagons and carts had to be completely dismantled, and the pieces were placed on two canoes strapped together. Stock animals swam alongside the canoes through the chilly waters.

As if to prove to settlers that rain was a permanent feature of the Oregon climate, the winter of 1851 brought extensive flooding, devastating developed areas of Springfield and destroying new homes. Yet the floods also had the unexpected benefit of indicating a natural

Ancient forests of Douglas fir provided building materials for the pioneers. Logging later became a major industry in the area. Photo courtesy of Photo Art Commercial Studios.

(right) The exhausting business of logging required cooperation, strength and stamina. Photo courtesy of the Springfield Museum.

canal from the middle fork of the Willamette River back to the main stem. Briggs and his father Isaac (or brother, according to some accounts), followed nature's design and dug a millrace using shovels and ox-drawn plows.

With the power available from the Springfield mill-race, Briggs embarked on his most ambitious venture yet. Borrowing the enormous sum of $10,000 from Albany millers Jeremiah Driggs and Thomas Monteith, the Briggses hired an experienced millwright from the east coast to design a sawmill and flour mill. Following the millwright's precise instructions, the Briggses constructed the mills in 1852. Powered by water wheels, both mills held some distinction in the area: the flour mill was the only mill of its kind in the county, and the sawmill provided the lumber for the first county courthouse. Drawing on the area's natural resources of abundant timber and fertile lands, the mills became the foundation for Springfield's industrial and economic growth.

Springfield began to develop a small commercial district in the 1850s. James Huddleston opened the first trading post in 1852 near the corner of present-day Mill and Main Streets. The following year J.N. Donalds took over the establishment. Springfield's business district grew along these two roads, and by 1860, a variety of artisans and professionals sold their goods and services there. Springfield residents on a shopping excursion would find a shoemaker, wagon maker, cabinet maker, four carpenters, two blacksmiths, a physician, and a merchant. A writer for the *Morning Oregonian* reported in 1864 that Springfield was "one of the busiest places he had seen."

In 1856, Springfield was platted, with two blocks between South A, Main, Mill, and Third Streets laid out into eight lots each. The lots measured 66 x 120 feet, and the town developed along a standard grid system oriented to the Willamette River. Also that year, the Dayton Treaty of 1856 removed the few remaining Kalapuya Indians to the small, crowded Grand Ronde Reservation north of Lane County. Many drifted away from the reservation and returned to the Springfield area.

Although economic development was foremost in the early settlers' minds, Springfield was more than farms and a few businesses. Springfield residents hastened to establish other community foundations, such as schools and churches. In 1854 the first school was erected. Agnes Stewart, a prim young woman of Scottish descent who came to the Valley from Pennsylvania with the famed Lost Wagon Train, was appointed the first teacher.

The small schoolhouse stood at the corner of South Seventh and B Streets, and although considered a "crude building," it served the community until the 1880s. Two new schools served residents in the Thurston area east of Springfield: the Davis School, built in the early 1850s, was a one-room schoolhouse at the east end of Thurston, and Thurston Elementary was established in the 1860s on the northeast corner of 66th and Thurston Road.

The McKenzie Forks Baptist Church was the first church in the Springfield area. Members of the congregation renamed it the First Baptist Church, and in 1871 they erected the first church building in Springfield at Second and C Streets, at a cost of $1600. The Springfield

Cougars constantly menaced the early pioneers and still roam the woods today. Here a dead cougar is propped up for an unusual photo. Photo courtesy of the Springfield Museum.

The millrace built by Elias and Isaac Briggs diverted water from the Willamette River and powered a succession of flour and lumber mills. Photo courtesy of the Springfield Museum.

Christian Church was founded in the late 1860s, with a meeting house built next to the original Pioneer Cemetery located at South 4th and C Streets sometime before 1880. In 1873, the denomination founded and ran a school.

In 1868, John H. Adams was appointed the first pastor of the newly-formed Methodist Church. The church lacked a building, so the First Baptist Church amicably shared its space. In 1881, the Methodists acquired a store building on Main Street for their activities, and in 1882, they began to hold week-long revival meetings on a yearly basis. In 1885, they built their own "new white" church with a parsonage beside it on the corner of Second and B Streets.

While Springfield was organizing itself into a proper town, Oregon Territory became a state in 1859, with a Lane County pioneer, John Whiteaker, installed as its pro-slavery governor. Abolitionists in Springfield and throughout the state disagreed with his politics, although after his single term in office he lived peacefully in nearby Pleasant Hill.

Because of the great distance and difficulties in travel between the Northwest and the East coast, few Oregonians fought in the Civil War, but sentiments ran deep and strong in the frontier state. Neighbors and friends were often at odds during the cataclysmic war.

Nevertheless, most residents apparently understood that cooperation was essential in promoting local development. With its commercial district, schools, and churches, Springfield might have seemed relatively bustling to the pioneers. Yet it remained a largely agrarian community. Census reports from 1850 and 1860 indicate that an overwhelming majority of the settlers engaged in agricultural endeavors. In approximately 1853, about 1000

acres were under cultivation in the Springfield area. Most of the farmers built up large herds of stock — cattle, oxen, horses, mules, sheep, and hogs — to take advantage of the open fields. They fenced smaller plots of 20 to 40 acres to cultivate wheat, oats, and vegetables for private use. Because of poor transportation and a lack of labor and equipment, few farmers initially raised grain crops for commercial purposes. However, the California Gold Rush provided the first major market for cereal grains, and Springfield farmers began to cultivate grain crops in addition to stock for outside markets.

In 1873, fourteen Springfield farmers formed the Springfield Grange No. 12, the first of its kind in Lane County. The Grange's primary goal in the West was to relieve Pacific Coast farmers from paying exorbitant prices for farm machinery and supplies, and to encourage buying and selling as a cooperative. Grange members also sought improved river transportation, free of monopolistic rate controls.

Indeed, transportation in Springfield and outlying areas in the mid-1800s was difficult. Early settlers assumed the Willamette River would provide easy transportation and access to outside markets, and Springfield looked to be the head of steamboat navigation. The settlers soon found the river surprisingly shallow, and only during floods could boats make it far enough upriver to reach Springfield. In a rare occurrence, heavy rains in 1861 deepened the Willamette enough for the steamer *Relief* to transport 13 tons of freight to Springfield. (In that same flood, residents had to travel through town in boats rather than by wagon.)

In 1871, the Oregon and California Railroad, building south from Portland, reached Lane County. Although the railroad originally planned to route the tracks through Springfield, a group of businessmen in nearby Eugene paid railroad financier Ben Holladay $48,000 to reroute the train through Eugene. The change was a blow to Springfield residents, who had looked forward to the certain growth that would accompany a railroad stop in town.

Springfield did make one advance in transportation in this period. In 1875, a covered wooden bridge, spanning 368 feet, replaced the Briggs Ferry. Probably nobody appreciated the bridge more than the animals that no longer had to swim across the river. Flooding swept away the bridge twice before 1891, and twice it was rebuilt with county funds and individual donations.

The mills that spurred Springfield's growth underwent changes of ownership in the 1860s. In 1864, Byron J. Pengra and a group of local businessmen founded the Springfield Manufacturing Company. Pengra was a unique figure in Springfield who served as Surveyor

General of the State, was a friend of Abraham Lincoln, and founded a pro-North newspaper, among other distinctive qualities. Because of his strongly expressed sentiments, he was known as "pugnacious Pengra."

In 1865, the company bought the sawmill and flour mill from the Briggses. The company rebuilt the sawmill, installing advanced new equipment, including a pair of double circular saws and a Leffel Turbinek wheel. It was considered the best mill in Lane County. In 1872, the shareholders of the company, probably concerned about the potential for growth after the railroad line chose Eugene over Springfield, sold the mills and water power to Pengra and his brother William.

By 1870, Springfield had grown to a population of 649. It had a post office, a commercial district, some of the best mills in the area, and well-established schools and churches. Although Springfield's growth slowed considerably after it was passed over by the railroad line, it continued to improve and expand as the new century drew near. ❶

IMPORTANT DATES:

1847/49:	Briggs Ferry established.
1851:	Briggses built Springfield millrace.
1852:	Briggses built sawmill and flour mill.
1854:	Springfield's first school.
1856:	Dayton Treaty removed Kalapuya Indians to Grande Ronde Reservation.
1865:	Springfield Manufacturing Company bought sawmill and flour mill.
1875:	New bridge across Willamette River replaced Briggs Ferry.

LOST WAGON TRAIN

In 1853, Elias Briggs and Mahlon Harlow, eager to attract new settlers and increase Springfield's population, sought an easier route to the Willamette Valley. They and other community leaders decided to build a cutoff from the Oregon Trail that would lead directly west to the Willamette Valley. Such a cutoff, called the Free Emigrant Road, would shorten the journey by 200 miles and avoid the difficult boat passage down the Columbia River.

Exploration parties set out to find the best routes, and by summer a road had been built through the Cascade Mountains. In July, a thirty-five-year-old settler from Kentucky named Elijah Elliot sent for his family and prepared to meet them on the Oregon Trail. He promised to spread word of the Free Emigrant Road and to lead a wagon train along the new route, although he himself had never seen or traveled it.

Elliot attracted approximately 1000 emigrants in 250 wagons, and he led them along the 1845 Meeks trail to Lake Harney, where it abruptly ended. The travelers were already low on provisions when they met Elliot, and by this time they were out of water and had almost no food remaining. Disoriented, they headed toward three peaks known as the Three Sisters, traveling through the cold desert without vegetation or water. Their animals died one after the other, and they cooked the meat and drank the blood for nourishment. When they reached the Deschutes River, they found road markers but no road. The group had to cut through thick forests on steep slopes, with everyone on foot because the wagons were continually tipping over.

Finally, one of the emigrants, Martin Blanding, went ahead for help. He made it to the small settlement of Lowell in the Willamette Valley, where residents were quick to offer assistance. Messengers rode through the valley calling for provisions, and settlers donated cattle and food staples. Search parties found the weary emigrants, fed them, and led them back to the Valley. Despite the hardships of the journey, many of the surviving travelers became prominent figures in Springfield and other communities.

Chapter
Three
3

BUDDING ENTERPRISE
1875-1899

While Springfield's growth slowed in the 1870s, the larger town of Eugene across the river assured its own future growth by aggressively campaigning for the siting of the University of Oregon. The university opened there in 1876 with one building, Deady Hall, and soon became the cultural center of the city, attracting numerous ancillary enterprises.

(above) Springfield's first school was a log cabin at South 7th and B Streets. The next school, first of several consecutive school houses built on Mill Street, is shown here in the 1880s, when it served about 69 students. Photo courtesy of the Springfield Museum. (right) Albert Shields Walker (1846-1915), Springfield's first mayor, was a popular blacksmith and civic leader. Photo courtesy of the Springfield Museum.

Paul Brattain came to Oregon from North Carolin in 1852. He served as Lane County clerk, auditor, and justice of the peace. Brattain School was named for him. Photo courtesy of the Springfield Museum.

(right) The C.W. Washburne family was well established in Springfield. The grandchildren are dressed in their finest for this photo. Photo courtesy of the Springfield Museum.

(right, below) At the Seavey hops yard in 1897 a large gathering of workers dressed up for a group photo. Photo courtesy of the Springfield Museum.

In spite of Springfield's slower growth, its citizens voted to incorporate their tiny city on February 25, 1885, and elected their popular blacksmith, 39-year-old Albert Shields Walker, as the first mayor. Other officials included Joseph W. Stewart, a merchant, as treasurer; W.R. Walker, a farmer, as city recorder; and councilmen T.O. Maxwell, owner of a livery stable, and William B. Pengra, mill owner and county surveyor.

Walker was a gregarious man who served four terms as mayor, as well as shoeing horses and repairing carriages in his establishment at Mill and Main Streets. He was also a member of the Board of Education, helped organize the First Methodist Church, and was Sunday School Superintendent for 20 years.

The first Council met in the Odd Fellows Hall, built in 1881 shortly after Springfield Lodge No. 70 of the I.O.O.F. was chartered with five founding members, among them Albert Walker. The Council soon passed an ordinance allowing the City to improve the streets by charging adjacent property owners, a common practice that elicits complaints to this day. Early in 1886 councilors set regulations governing the sale of "spiritous or malt liquors," and listed as offenses disorderly conduct, gambling, opium smoking, splitting wood on the sidewalk, and keeping a bawdy house.

The small city's commercial influence extended to the lush green farms surrounding the city. In the 1880s, hops began to replace wheat as a major commercial crop, especially after Alexander Seavey established his beautiful farm along the McKenzie River in 1877. Peppermint and flax also gained importance.

In his 1884 book, *Illustrated History of Lane County, Oregon,* Albert G. Walling wrote, "There is more wealth

among the farmers of this district than can be found
in any other portion of Lane County . . . There is not an
acre of valley land in Springfield precinct unoccupied."

Although the number of farms increased, their average
size diminished to about 212 acres, and often that acreage
was under water. As the farmers saw it, another decade,
another major flood. After the wooden wagon bridge
over the Willamette was washed out at least twice by
1891, a sturdy steel bridge with a 400-foot span replaced
it at the cost of $40,000. By then frequent stagecoaches
crossed the bridge, with regular service between
Springfield and Eugene, as well as trips to Foley Springs,
Lowell, and Mabel.

In 1891 Collis P. Huntington finally brought the
Southern Pacific Railroad to Springfield by way of Coburg
and extending to Natron. The Springfield Investment
and Power Company donated land on the southern edge
of the city for the site of a handsome Stick Chalet-style
depot. Now Springfield could trade more easily with the
rest of the country, and a grand celebration, complete
with red, white, and blue bunting and a brass band,
marked the arrival of the first train.

A Western Union telegraph office opened in the depot,
and instant communications spanned the continent. In
the next two decades businesses in Springfield multiplied,
and lumber companies were able to operate on a large
scale. Prosperity for the common worker seemed guaranteed.

Confidence in the future encouraged investment.
Although Byron Pengra's aging sawmill burned down in
1882, he replaced it with an even larger three-story mill,
which he sold in 1884 to Almon Wheeler. The new owner
succeeded so well that the demand for high-grade lumber
soon exceeded the mill's capacity. Wheeler expanded the
mill in 1891, producing lumber of red and yellow fir,
spruce, hemlock, and cedar, including fine moldings.

In 1890 Charles W. Washburne, a Junction City
banker, bought William Pengra's flour mill and installed
new machinery that increased production to 150 barrels
of flour a day. With Washburne's son Byron in charge
of operations, the mill gained renown throughout
the Northwest for its high-quality flour named
"Snowball XXX."

In a town built almost entirely of wood, fire was just
as disastrous, and just as regular, as flooding. Springfield

organized its first volunteer fire department in the 1890s. Known as the "Hook, Ladder, and Bucket Brigade," it operated out of the ever-useful Odd Fellows Hall. Hand-pumped hose carts, pulled by running firefighters, rushed to every reported fire.

As soon as a business or home burned down, it was usually rebuilt. Construction of new buildings was even more evident. When residents learned that the railroad would be coming to Springfield, they knew that visitors needed a place to stay. Springfield's first hotel, the Clark Hotel, sprang up on Mill Street in 1890. Around 1891 the large wooden Springfield Hotel was built on Main Street, where it remained a landmark until 1959.

The City Council provided for new sidewalks in 1892, a much-needed amenity in such a muddy town. Chickens, ducks, and an occasional hog still strolled along Mill and Main Streets like any other citizen.

"I can remember back as far as 1884. Springfield was just a wide place in the road."
Frank Withers, 1979 Oral History Project

Nevertheless, the 1890s were paving the way for the new century, and eventually even the roads would be paved.

Springfielders considered their town properly established when it acquired a City Charter on March 17, 1893. Downtown consisted of general stores and service providers, the two hotels, two undertaking parlors, two real estate-insurance businesses, two photographers, a travel agent, two druggists, a physician, two newspapers, and the Baptist, Methodist, and other Christian churches.

By this time, culture was coming to town, even a bit of refinement. In 1892, the brothers W.F. (Frank) and W.G. (Will) Gilstrap published a weekly newspaper called *The*

Springfielders prepare for a holiday trip to the coast. Approximately 70 miles, the journey took as long as a week. The black bloomers worn by two of the women were considered "vulgar." Photo courtesy of the Springfield Museum.

Springfield Messenger for about a year. The Gilstraps set and printed the local news on a hand press. John Kelly started a newspaper called the *Nonpareil* in 1896. Within two years he sold the business to John F. Woods, who later changed its name to *The Springfield News*. The newspaper changed ownership numerous times over the years, but still provides Springfielders with the local news.

Springfield's education system was limited to a one-room school until the 1880s, when a new two-room schoolhouse was built at Mill and D Streets. By 1888 the school had become crowded with 67 students (many without shoes), and in 1889 the building was sawed in half and moved onto D Street, where the two parts served as private residences.

At the Mill Street site the school district built a new two-room, two-story school complete with belfry, wood stove, and an outside drinking fountain. After it became too crowded, the younger students attended classes in a former cheese factory on Mill Street. By 1891 the student population mushroomed to 120, due in part, no doubt, to the influx of businesses and workers stimulated by the railroad. High school instruction began in 1897 with perhaps a dozen students.

Music was considered both educational and entertaining, and Springfield's Cornet Band was organized in 1889 with Tim Wheeler as director. The band performed regularly in a bandstand on the southwest corner of Second and Main Streets in a grove of locust trees. This was probably Springfield's first park, where people gathered not only for concerts but for barbecues and ice cream socials. By 1892 a baseball team played visiting teams at a diamond between 5th and 7th and B and Main Streets.

By now the town was developing more along Main Street than on Mill Street. The first opera house, built in 1893, was used by local performers and touring companies, which presented popular plays, variety shows, and vaudeville. Real opera was probably rarely heard. The grand opening featured a performance by the Springfield Band, led by G. H. Veringler, with a tuba solo performed by one of the owners of the *Messenger*, and the "Levy Athan Polka," played by the felicitously named Oliver C. Purkeypile, Southern Pacific station master. Admission to the show was 25 cents.

As the new century approached, so did a brand-new enterprise, the Booth-Kelly Lumber Company. Its founders were Robert A. Booth, his brother Henry, and George and Tom Kelly, sons of John F. Kelly, who had an interest in the early Springfield Manufacturing Company. These respected and successful citizens (Booth was a state senator at the time), incorporated their lumber company in 1895. The company built the mill

town of Wendling on the Mohawk River northeast of Springfield in 1899, the same year that Southern Pacific erected Hayden Bridge across the McKenzie River.

Railroading and more modern mills and logging techniques were about to transform Springfield into a true mill town, one that far surpassed Elias Briggs' greatest expectations when he arrived half a century earlier. But as the century drew to a close, Briggs was in no condition to understand the significance of the town he founded. He died on January 17, 1896 in Salem, Oregon, where he resided at the Oregon State Hospital, the state insane asylum. He was buried in a field next to the hospital. ✿

IMPORTANT DATES:

1882:   Sawmill burned down and was replaced with larger mill.
1885:   City of Springfield incorporated.
1891:   Southern Pacific Railroad added depot in Springfield, complete with a Western Union telegraph office.
1893:   Springfield acquired City Charter.
1895:   Booth-Kelly lumber mill established.
1899:   Southern Pacific Railroad erected Hayden Bridge over McKenzie River.

DOUGLAS GARDENS

Samuel M. Douglas, who came to the area in 1888, built up one of Springfield's largest and most prosperous farms, purchasing over 1,000 acres above the flood plain between what is now 32nd Street and 42nd Street, and from McKenzie Highway to the Willamette River.

Douglas and his wife Florence operated a large dairy, cured meat, and grew produce. In a time before farms had electricity, his modern equipment was steam run. When the railroad to Natron was built on his land in 1891, Douglas gained a flag stop at 32nd Street in exchange for the right-of-way. He had the right to stop any train and load it with cream, cheese, and butter for shipment to Portland.

Samuel Douglas's mother was Lucinda Hanks, a first cousin of Nancy Hanks, Abraham Lincoln's mother, and his father was a first cousin of Lincoln's rival, Senator Stephen A. Douglas. The lovely Douglas house stands to this day.

Samuel, Sadie and Florence Douglas about 1900. Samuel Douglas was one of the most innovative and prosperous farmers in the area. Photo courtesy of the Springfield Museum.

(following page) The McKenzie Stage transported passengers up the McKenzie Highway, part of which was a toll road. Photo courtesy of the Springfield Museum.

EARLY THURSTON

The area known as Thurston, which now comprises the eastern part of Springfield, began to be settled just a few years after Springfield. We're not sure how Thurston got its name. We do know that in 1851 John McNutt, an Irish immigrant, recorded the first donation land claim in the area, roughly between what is now 58th Street, 66th Street, Main Street, and Thurston Road. In 1855 his younger brother David took a claim north of his.

Some other early settlers were also foreign born, including Isaac Whittaker of Germany, his wife Anna Mary of either Germany or Switzerland, along with their two American-born sons, James and Isaac. Anna Mary's Swiss-born son John Kizer joined them later. Other settlers came from various states, including William Y. Miller, a physician from Kentucky, and his wife Sarah.

In the 1850s Nelson Davis donated land for the Davis School. The Thurston Elementary School, built in the 1860s, served until 1930. Located at 66th Street (then called Russell Road) and Thurston Road, the school was right in the heart of the sparse commercial district. Nearby was the Thurston Post Office, established in 1877 by Dr. B.F. Russell, whose home later became the county poor farm.

The Thurston Church of Christ was organized in 1890 with 132 members, and in 1893 Martin and Martha Rees donated land for a church building. Thurston became a convenient stagecoach stop for travelers heading east, and passengers could spend the night in rooms above the general store.

Farmers considered Thurston's river-bottom soil first rate for growing wheat, hay, and hops. Huge old maples grew in the area, and in the 1890s William Jasper Billings used the lovely wood to create a small industry making lathed bowls and kitchen utensils.

Throughout Thurston's early history, Indians left the reservations and returned to camp in the area during good weather. They fished on the McKenzie River near Hendrick's Bridge, and earned cash by picking hops and working as field hands.

Chapter Four

REACHING OUTWARD
1900-1911

The turn of the century ushered in a new era in Springfield. The early 1900s saw tremendous changes locally, from the development of major new industries to the modernization of technology and facilities. Springfield entered the twentieth century as a muddy little town, but it soon came into its own as a thriving industrial center. In the first years of the new century residents marveled at the advent of telephone service, indoor plumbing, and electricity supplied by competing firms.

(above) Street improvement at the early part of the century already required heavy equipment. Workers here are smoothing Franklin Boulevard in Glenwood. Photo courtesy of the Springfield Museum. (right) The Prune Hill flume provided another way of transporting logs downhill. When people slid down it for fun, it was as exciting as a roller coaster ride, and far more dangerous. Photo courtesy of the Springfield Museum.

Perhaps nothing transformed Springfield more in the twentieth century than the introduction of several new industries that spurred the city's economic growth and attracted new settlers. Although Springfield remained a largely agrarian community at the turn of the century, Springfield farmers soon developed more sophisticated (and lucrative) approaches to agriculture in the early 1900s, specializing in crops that were well suited to the Willamette Valley climate and soil.

A splash dam on the McKenzie River in 1905 allowed loggers to control the flow of the water when floating logs down the river. Photo courtesy of the Springfield Museum.

(right) The Booth-Kelly Lumber Company built the nearby company town of Wendling as a base for loggers and their families east of Springfield. The Booth-Kelly train hauled massive logs over private rails to the Springfield station. Wendling residents often hitched a ride into town. Photos courtesy of the Springfield Museum.

One such crop was hops, whose pungent flower was used in beer made in German breweries in Portland and Vancouver, Washington. Thousands of acres of hops were planted in the Springfield area, making Oregon the leading producer of hops in the country. The hop harvest season, which typically began in late August or early September and lasted three to four weeks, engaged much of the farming community. Most local farmers were largely self-sufficient, but they needed cash to buy staples and services. Hop-picking was a convenient way to earn a good portion of their income for the year.

Picking hops was a family affair. Children picked alongside their parents, and at a pay rate of one cent per pound, an industrious family could return home with a hearty sum of money. Clair Cooley, who helped his parents pick hops when he was a young boy, recalled in an article in the *Lane County Historian* that his mother could earn as much as eight dollars per day.

The pickers all stayed in tents or wooden shelters on the hop farms, sleeping in rows of bunkbeds. Many of the families were already friends with one another, and the experience was so sociable that Cooley described it as a "paid vacation." Saturday night dances fostered romances and friendships.

Many hop growers, such as John Seavey and H.L. Edmunson, welcomed Native Americans from the Warm Springs reservation as pickers. The Native Americans usually pitched their own tents on the farm, which other pickers called the Indian Camp. Other growers were partial to Hawaiians, who provided evening entertainment for the pickers with Island songs and dances.

In addition to hops, Springfield became the nation's first producer of filberts, or hazelnuts, thanks to an enterprising couple named George and Luella (Lulu) Dorris. A lawyer by training, George Dorris decided to try his hand at farming when he bought a 277-acre property from George Thurston in 1892. Located half a mile south of Springfield at the confluence of the Middle and Coast Forks of the Willamette River, Dorris' property became the site of much experimentation. Dorris planted hops, fruit, and various vegetables but had little success. At the turn of the century, the owner of a California nursery convinced him that filbert trees would grow like blackberries in the sandy soil of his new farm, and Dorris bought 50 trees of a type that originated in Barcelona, Spain.

He sold his first harvests throughout the United States to communities of European immigrants, who were more familiar with the nuts than Americans. Dorris developed technologically advanced methods for growing hazelnuts, and the farm continued to produce hazelnuts under the management of his nephew, Ben, for nearly 70 years.

Dorris encouraged other local farmers to plant hazelnut trees, laying the foundation for Oregon's hazelnut industry that remains strong to this day. The Dorrises created the Dorris Ranch Nursery, which operated for 40 years and produced approximately 70,000 trees annually for new orchards around the country. Half of all the commercial hazelnut trees growing in the U.S. today originated from Dorris Ranch nursery stock.

In 1972, through the generosity of Ben and Kay Dorris, the Dorris Ranch was acquired by Willamalane Park and Recreation District, which turned the Ranch into a living history farm, and still sells 75 acres' worth of hazelnuts each year.

Around 1900 Mrs. Peter Benson outfitted a home on the north side of Main Street between Mill and Second Streets as Springfield's first hospital. The Springfield Private Hospital opened for business about the same time that the lumber industry, with its many dangers, was poised for enormous growth.

In 1901, Springfield's lumber industry took flight when the Booth-Kelly Company purchased the Springfield sawmill and 70,000 acres of timberland in the region. The company dismantled the old sawmill and replaced it with a larger mill featuring cutting-edge

Loggers pause for a photo during the dangerous job of floating logs downstream. Photo courtesy of the Springfield Museum.

(top) The Thurston Post Office was a center of activity in the settlement east of Springfield. Thurston eventually was annexed to Springfield. Photo courtesy of the Springfield Museum.

The Booth-Kelly Mill was not the only example of advanced technology in Springfield in the early 1900s. In the true spirit of the Progressive era, Springfield residents devoted their energies to modernizing and improving life in the twentieth century. By 1903, telephones had come to Springfield, with both local and long distance service available. In 1906, the city had 38 telephones on the exchange. As part of sanitizing efforts, Springfield had a public water system installed by the Willamette Valley Company in 1906. A bond issue to build sewers was passed the next year. The cost of water was fifty cents a month for faucet, bathtub, and water closet facilities. For many satisfied residents, that meant no more trips to the outhouse through the mud and rain.

Springfield also witnessed major advances in transportation in the early 1900s. Stagecoach travel increased to include regular stops in Thurston, Walterville, and Leaburg. Springfield travelers could go even farther by railroad. The Southern Pacific Railroad built a steel railroad bridge across the Willamette in 1906, giving Springfield rail service to Eugene and Portland.

In 1910, Springfield welcomed the Portland, Eugene, and Eastern Railway's electric streetcars, which were touted as faster, cheaper, and cleaner than trains and stage. A $30,000 bridge was built specifically for the streetcars under the direction of Lord Nelson Roney. The first streetcar crossed the bridge from Eugene to Springfield on Saturday, October 22, 1910, and was met by a jubilant crowd. *The Eugene Daily Guard* reported dramatically that as Springfield residents eagerly awaited sight of the first streetcar, a "cheer broke from the waiting crowd, and as Horatius reaching the far shore of the Tiber, the yellow cars came down from the approach of the bridge into Springfield amid noise and confusion." The streetcar ran up Main Street to 10th Street, replacing the less comfortable stagecoach as the primary mode of transportation between Springfield and Eugene.

The streetcar was busy transporting Eugene drinkers after Eugene opted to become a "dry" community, rendering Springfield the only "wet" location between Salem and Oakland. Soon there were nine saloons in Springfield, outnumbering the churches in town. A sheriff rode the streetcar on Saturday evenings to protect lady passengers from unruly drunks.

Springfield's growth also was reflected in the many new businesses established in the early 1900s. The city's first Chamber of Commerce organized with 25 members in 1904. On January 1, 1904, the first bank

production technology. The new mill, which cost $250,000 to build, employed a total of 1000 workers and could cut 250,000 board feet a day. In 1903 the Booth-Kelly Mill had its most productive year, producing more than 143-million board feet.

Springfield's population, which stood at 353 in 1900, multiplied to nearly 2,000 by 1910. Half of the entire Springfield community worked at the Booth-Kelly Mill. Market conditions boosted the industry even further. Lumber sales rose dramatically during the Alaska gold rush between 1900 and 1903, and again after the 1906 San Francisco earthquake.

The old sawmill had been powered by a steam plant built adjacent to the millrace. Since this fuel exceeded the needs of the new, more efficient mill, the Booth-Kelly Company was granted a franchise to furnish electric power to a new light plant in Springfield, run by the Eugene Electric Light Company. In addition, Booth-Kelly built a large mill pond to store logs on the western half of the millrace.

in Springfield opened with a capital of $20,000 and was named, appropriately, First Bank. Located in a tiny wooden structure on Main Street, its president was E.E. Kepner. Two years later the First National Bank opened for business about a block away, with Cy Brattain as president. Shortly after opening, the First National bought out the First Bank.

Several fraternal organizations also emerged in this period. The Springfield Grange No. 378 was established in 1908, with 95 charter members. In 1910, the Master Woodsmen's Lodge of Springfield was formed, with a lodge hall on Main Street. The I.O.O.F. erected a substantial building in 1909.

The school system continued to expand as well. Between 1907 and 1912, the Mill Street school was enlarged and converted into a high school. Maple School organized around 1895, Mt. Vernon School opened

around 1900, and Lincoln Elementary and Hayden Bridge Schools were built about 1910. The schools lost an important figure, however, when Springfield's first teacher, Agnes Stewart Warner, died in 1905. A public library was established in 1908 and stocked books in City Hall and First National Bank during its early years.

Springfield residents did more than work and study, however, and a number of new businesses provided entertainment for the community. In 1907, a skating rink

---

"The only transportation we had from Springfield to Wendling was the railroad for a good many years. Till cars come into use, and then the road was no good. We could only go in the summertime. But we had good railroad service. We had five trains a day."
Herschel "Curley" Bailey, 1979 Oral History Project

(opposite page, below) By 1911, train tracks connecting Springfield to Eugene ran right down the center of Main Street, which was paved later that year. The streetcar proved hugely successful, allowing Springfielders to shop conveniently in Eugene, and Eugeneans to drink in Springfield's saloons. Photo courtesy of the Springfield Museum.

(left) This downtown cigar store, shown around 1910, provided men with an alternative to the watering holes as a place to discuss the city's business. Photo courtesy of the Springfield Museum.

opened on Main Street and later moved to a site on the river on South D Street. That same year a popular play performance at the Opera House was *For Love's Sake*, advertised as "a military drama with plenty of action." In 1910, the Bell Theatre was built. To read about all these activities, Springfield residents continued to consult *The Springfield News*, which had been established in 1903, and operated out of the ever-popular Odd Fellows Hall.

With plentiful jobs and firmly established community institutions in the early 1900s, Springfield had laid the groundwork to meet the many challenges the new century would bring. Yet Springfielders would soon discover that their newfound prosperity was fragile, and that disaster might always be around the corner.

Despite the efficiency and technology of the new Booth-Kelly Mill, it was no match for an age-old foe of all edifices: fire. In July 1911, the grand mill began to bellow smoke and flames. Within 15 minutes, the blaze enveloped a dozen acres of lumber and the building was beyond repair. In the direct path of the fire stood an oil storage tank that could decimate the town of Springfield if it exploded. Disaster was barely averted when a railroad engineer raced to Junction City to load a steam pump that could pump water from the millrace onto the oil storage tank. The town, just when it could taste prosperity, had lost its livelihood. ❶

IMPORTANT DATES:

1892:	George Dorris bought property that became Dorris Ranch.
1900:	Springfield's first hospital, Springfield Private Hospital, opened.
1901:	Booth-Kelly purchased and dismantled sawmill, and built larger mill.
1903:	*Springfield News* established.
1903:	Telephone service became available.
1906:	Public water system installed by Willamette Valley Company.
1910:	Springfield acquired electric streetcars.
1911:	Booth-Kelly mill burned down.

(right, top) In the early 1900s the northeast corner of Mill and A Streets was the busiest spot in town. Owner of the popular Mt. Hood Saloon was William L. McFarland, seen here on crutches. Photo courtesy of the Springfield Museum.

(right, below) Springfield's first hospital opened around 1900 on Main Street. Photo courtesy of the Springfield Museum.

On hops picking:
"I could never pick more than 100 or 150. I guess as I got older I could get near 200 pounds. There was a few women who talked just as fast as could be and picked just as fast, and they got about 300 pounds. And in the evenings, they'd have dances, and taffy pulls and all kinds of things going. It was kind of a lark, visiting and fun evenings and we got away from home a while."
Marjorie Colpitts, 1979 Oral History Project

(right) Early students at Mt. Vernon School often attended classes barefoot. Photo courtesy of the Springfield Museum.

(below) Springfield's baseball team in good-looking uniforms, 1910. A succession of baseball teams competed against other teams throughout the state. Photo courtesy of the Springfield Museum.

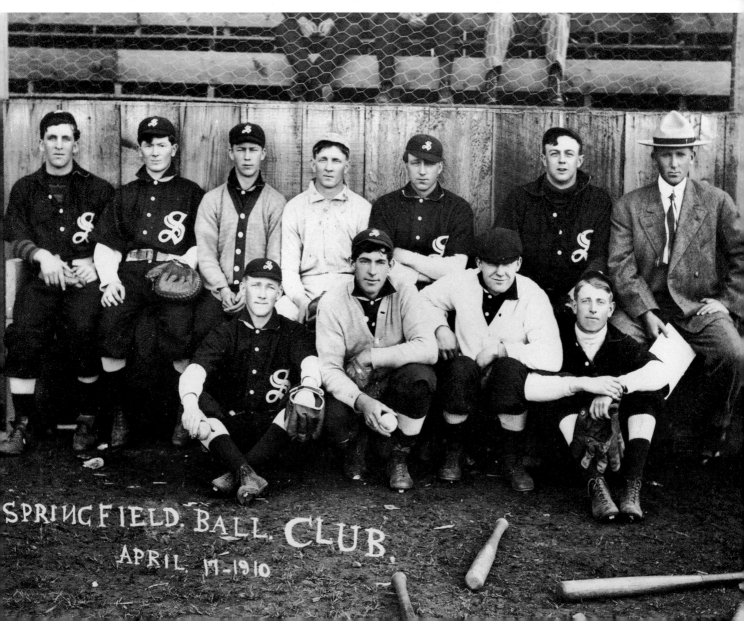

SPRINGFIELD BALL CLUB. APRIL 17-1910

(left) The Douglas house was surrounded by lovely acreage when it was built. It is still one of Springfield's finest historical homes. Photo courtesy of the Springfield Museum.

(below) The Edwin Meach home is typical of the wooden structures in the Washburne District, a historical residential area. Most of the homes in the working-class neighborhood were built between 1890 and 1930. Photo courtesy of the Springfield Museum.

THE PHOENIX RISES
1911-1930

The Booth-Kelly fire left half the town suddenly unemployed.

Yet Springfielders did not let this tragedy stand in the way of progress.

The pioneer spirit that had created Springfield held strong in the twenti-

eth century and was evident in the economic growth and community

enhancement that the town sustained through the 1920s.

(above) Some of Springfield's leading business people in the early part of the century. Molly Seavey, Gus Washburne, Ambrose Middleton, Maude Bryan, L.M. Beebe, John C. Mullen, Maud Beebe, Isaac Larimer, Mrs. Middleton, Jess Seavey, Sadie Perkins, Joe Bryan, Mrs. Machen, Mrs. Bell, Manda Washburne, Edythe Larimer, Al Perkins, John Bell, Jack Machen, Dorene Larimer, Crystal Bryan, Alene Larimer, Frank Beebe, Junior Bell and Earl Beebe. Photo courtesy of the Springfield Museum. (right) The February 1927 flood devastated the entire city. Photo courtesy of the Springfield Museum.

GLENWOOD

Despite the trauma of the fire, Springfield residents forged ahead with their efforts to modernize and refine the town's living conditions. Springfield's muddy streets were littered with rubbish and lumber, and the sidewalks were rutted and uneven. In 1911, the city sponsored a program entitled "Permanent Improvement," which aimed to improve and beautify Springfield streets.

Clarence Virway, Robert Rule, Guy Noble and Buck Beadle, probably during World War I. Photo courtesy of the Springfield Museum.

The pinnacle of Permanent Improvement's accomplishments came in the summer of 1911, when Main Street was paved from Mill to 10th. Citizens celebrated the event in October of that year with a masquerade ball on the new thoroughfare, complete with speeches, dancing, two brass bands, and a procession led by Mayor W.M. Sutton. The theme was "Springfield Paves the Way."

The lumber industry was only temporarily slowed by the mill fire. In 1912, Booth-Kelly rebuilt the mill, and its 1,000 employees returned to work. In addition to the new mill, Booth-Kelly built a railroad that year to serve the many logging camps in the Springfield area. The Booth-Kelly Mill suffered another small fire in 1915, but it recovered quickly.

While Booth-Kelly remained the lumber giant in the Springfield timber industry, other lumber mills also operated in the area. The 1921 city directory documents "large lumber manufacturing mills, sash, door, and planing mill, barrel stave factory, shingle mill, and lesser industrial manufactories" as sources of employment for Springfield residents. That same year, a factory for making portable houses and garages opened in an old planing mill building. In 1919, the Thurston area acquired its only sawmill, when George Williams dug a millrace connecting a natural backwater of the McKenzie River with Cedar Flat Creek and built a mill there. He operated the mill until 1936.

Although a number of Springfield's young men went off to fight in World War I, Springfield's major industries benefited from the war. The disaster created a European market for both timber and hops that lasted long after peace was

(above) Smith Mountjoy was well known locally in the early part of the century as a photographer and an avid aficionado of motorcycles. Photo courtesy of the Springfield Museum.

(left) The Moose Lodge is represented by this unique vehicle in the Fourth of July parade, 1916. The Springfield Livery Stable stood at Main and Mill Streets, the former location of Albert Walker's blacksmith shop. Photo courtesy of the Springfield Museum.

declared. By 1929, 55 percent of the hops exported by the United States came from Oregon.

The Springfield flour mill went through numerous permutations in the early 1900s. It was sold several times after the 1915 death of owner C.W. Washburne, until George Bushman and Sons purchased the operation in 1919, renaming it the Springfield Mill and Grain Company. Fire destroyed the business in 1930, and a new flour mill was never built. On the site of the old mill now stands the Borden Company, a producer of glues for secondary wood processing.

Other industries also emerged in Springfield in this period. A meat-packing plant opened in 1920, and a tannery and second meat plant were in operation by 1926. The Springfield Creamery opened around 1911 on 3rd Street (now Pioneer Parkway) between Main and North A Streets. Creameries typically were located in the center of town, where all the farmers brought their milk. The Springfield Creamery produced mainly cheese at first, and later added space for processing milk. By the mid-1950s, the creamery produced mostly ice cream and was acquired by Darigold.

Springfield's boosters promoted its deserved image of rich farming and fruit country in this period and it continued to develop agriculturally. Farm products marketed in the 1920s included livestock, wool, wheat, oats, hay, and vegetables. Springfield also gained acclaim for its many farms that grew Angora goats for the mohair industry. By 1920, 39 dairies existed in Springfield, and by the 1930s, 86 poultry breeders operated in the area.

Springfield was home to several successful commercial fruit orchards around 1918. By 1934, 38 growers in the area produced a variety of fruits, including cherries, berries, apples, peaches, and pears. In addition to the filbert industry spawned by Dorris Ranch, walnuts became a major crop in Springfield. The Hayden Bridge Road and Game Farm Road areas were the sites of several walnut orchards, remnants of which exist today.

The Thurston area remained largely rural in this period, and it produced a good deal of Springfield's agricultural output beginning around 1928. Poultry breeders, dairies, fruit growers, and livestock breeders comprised Thurston's substantial farming community. The area even had its own prune-drying plant.

Springfield also became a national producer of bulbs and flowers in the 1920s. Flowering bulbs were raised in

Overview of Springfield looking southeast from Kelly Butte, April 1915. Photo courtesy of the Springfield Museum.

Bailey recalled Springfield before it adopted prohibition in 1915.

"I came from Coburg to Springfield on the train one night about midnight. It was just before the saloons closed up. And down Main Street in Springfield the streetcar could hardly get by for drunks running up and down the street. That's how rough it was."

Herschel "Curley" Bailey, 1979 Oral History Project

the Gateway area, and Chase Gardens was cultivating flowers by 1925. The large-scale Chase operation grew potted plants, carnations, roses, and orchids, until the Depression stifled the market for such luxuries. Bartholomew Gardens supplied produce to the lumber camps and the urban area.

Although the town still had a large agrarian element, Springfield took on a distinctly modern air in the 1920s as the automobile became more commonplace. The first automobile arrived in Springfield in 1907, and by 1911 Springfield had an auto dealership called Gittins and Bally. The advent of the "horseless carriage" required some adjustment on the part of the Springfielders. Local blacksmiths learned to become auto mechanics or went out of business. The streetcar, which had seemed a glorious advancement in 1911, was outdated by the 1920s. In 1926 streetcar service was discontinued and replaced by bus service.

Several businesses that catered to auto owners emerged in the 1920s. A garage (for auto repair) is listed in the 1915 city directory, and a service station was opened in the 1920s by Ernest Black. By 1928, the Thurston area also acquired a service station. That same year, Springfield had two automobile dealers, three service stations, and a taxicab service.

The popularity of automobiles in Springfield was evident in 1929, when the city decided to replace the celebrated streetcar bridge across the Willamette with a span of concrete and steel for vehicle use, the same bridge that now carries west-bound traffic from Main Street. The remains of the old streetcar bridge can be seen in the cement piers in the river at South A Street. In 1921, the McKenzie Highway became a part of a state highway network, connecting Springfield to the eastern part of the state.

Springfielders used their new automobiles to travel to the many retail and service businesses in Springfield in this era. Between 1907 and 1921, the number of businesses in Springfield grew from 34 to 96. Springfield residents could find nearly any modern amenity they desired in the city's downtown, which was home to several banks and hotels, a publishing house, and a number of specialty

shops, including a watchmaker, tailor, and floral shop. In 1914, W.J. Hills opened Hills Department Store.

A popular candy shop and soda fountain, Eggimann's Candy Kitchen, was the center of social activity from at least 1919 to the 1940s. Eggimann's candies were shipped throughout the state. C.F. Eggimann served as mayor from 1921-25, and his wife Myrtle acted as surrogate mother to every youngster who came through the door.

In 1915, saloon owners had to find a new line of work when the Mayor declared prohibition in Springfield. Springfield residents likely found their new automobiles handy to drive to their favorite watering holes in Eugene, which had gone "wet" in 1913. The entire state went "bone dry" by signature of Governor James Whithycombe in February 1917, two years before Prohibition became federal law.

Although Springfield was a well-established town of more than 60 years by this period, its pioneer heritage was reinforced in the 1920s by an influx of Ukrainian immigrants. A group of Ukrainian families, most of them farmers who had lost their homesteads in North Dakota, relocated in the rural areas of Springfield. The first Ukrainian settlers, pleased with their new homes in the Willamette Valley, encouraged their relatives to join them, forming a Ukrainian community which still exists today.

The explosion of economic growth in Springfield fostered the expansion of schools, churches, and other community institutions. In 1921, the first high school was razed and replaced with a new building, which today serves as the Administration Building. Brattain Elementary School was established in 1925, bringing the district's totals up to 772 students and 31 teachers.

The Methodist Church, one of the first churches established in Springfield, had a membership of 304

*"They had a big bunk house and cook house and a lot of
fellows that had families in Springfield worked up through
the week and then come home on the train on the weekend.
We lived in a tent at the logging camp. And pack rats
came in and carried the silverware off."*
Edythe Laxton, 1979 Oral History Project

---

parishioners by 1916. That year, Miss Margaret Morris
offered the church $15,000 to erect a new church build-
ing in memory of her uncle, James Armstrong Ebbert,
providing it was renamed the Ebbert Memorial United
Methodist Church. The offer was accepted and the completed building still stands at 532 C Street. The striking
new church, with a brick veneer, was designed by Albert
Crandall, an architect from Lebanon, Oregon. Its most
distinctive feature is the 23 stained-glass windows, 13 on
the main floor and 10 on the second floor, manufactured
by the Povey Brothers of Portland. The new building
incorporated the old church's bell in the southeast tower.

In 1912, the city officially designated Springfield's first
public library in the City Hall building on Main Street,
and Mayor Welby Stevens appointed the first library
board that same year. Springfield's City Hall, which
stood on Main Street by at least 1909, also housed
the fire department equipment: two hose carts with
a 500 foot hose in each, and one hook and ladder truck.
The big fire bell remains in City Hall today. Behind City
Hall stood Springfield's tiny "calaboose," the old western
term for jail.

In 1913, Thurston area residents built the Thurston
Community Hall across from the general store on
Thurston Road. The Community Hall has the distinction
of being one of the first buildings in Oregon to be constructed with curved laminated beams that form an arched
roof and ceiling. The Hall served as the social center for
Thurston, and was used for classes, dances, theatre,
sports, and public meetings, much as it operates today.

Springfield General Hospital, the city's second hospital, opened in 1914 on F Street. Run by a nurse, Hazel
Adrian, the hospital served the community until 1936,
when the building was remodeled into apartments. The
building stands today as Pollard House Apartments,
named after Dr. W. H. Pollard, one of the hospital's most
distinguished physicians. The hospital treated many
of the Springfield residents infected with the Spanish flu
in 1918, which affected people in epidemic proportions
worldwide. Perhaps some of them convalesced in the
Pest House, a cottage behind the hospital that was
used to isolate patients with contagious diseases.

After the Booth-Kelly fire, World War I, and the
Spanish flu epidemic, Springfield proved that it could
survive a series of disasters and continue the march
toward progress. It would need that hardy pioneer spirit
once again in 1929 when the stock market crashed and
hard times hit the nation. ◗

(right) A tiny trailer held everything needed for an extended camping trip. Photo courtesy of the Springfield Museum.

(below) In the early days of motoring, camping out was a lot more primitive than it is today. Photo courtesy of the Springfield Museum.

IMPORTANT DATES:

1911: City sponsored program to improve Springfield's streets entitled "Permanent Improvement."

1911: Main Street paved from Mill to 10th Streets.

1912: City officially designated Springfield's first public library in City Hall.

1912: Booth-Kelly rebuilt mill.

1915: Prohibition declared in Springfield.

1926: Streetcars replaced with bus service.

Edythe Laxton's father served as an informal banker, cashing the workers' checks.
"My dad paid them in gold. If there had been any rowdiness up at camp, Dad always dug a hole in the yard and buried the box of money."
Edythe Laxton, 1979 Oral History Project

Crystal Fogle's parents ran the first movie theatre.
"They had signs on the sides asking men not to spit on the floor and for women to remove their hats. If any of the young people got boisterous in the theatre, Father stopped the program, came down the aisle, straightened them out, and we had order in the theatre."
Crystal Fogle, 1979 Oral History Project

The Ladies Civic Club paid for this arch in West Springfield as a welcome to tourists. Springfield was known as the "Gateway to the McKenzie River." Photo courtesy of the Springfield Museum.

BOOTH-KELLY SAW MILL & YARD BURNING Springfield Ore. JULY 28th 1911.

(above) An enterprising photographer quickly produced postcards with this view of the Booth-Kelly mill fire. Photo courtesy of the Springfield Museum.

(left) A day in the country could include a crossing on a wobbly extension bridge. Photo courtesy of the Springfield Museum.

SPRINGFIELD ORE.

#8

Chapter Six

SURVIVING CHAOS
1930-1960

As the nation sank into the Great Depression, the economic growth of Springfield slowed to a crawl. Although Springfield fared better than some other parts of the country, work became scarce and Springfielders struggled to make ends meet.

(above) The old McKenzie Pass Highway in 1946. The old highway still serves as a scenic route to the mountains of central Oregon in the summers. Photo courtesy of the Springfield Museum. (right) Ray Nott's garage on the north side of Mail Street about 1937. Left to right: Paul Leroy Nott, Norris Schurtevoigne, Ray William Nott and Neil Pellard. On right are neighboring barbers, Harry Whitney and Clark Wheaton. Photo courtesy of the Springfield Museum.

The effects of the Depression were felt in every home throughout Springfield. The Booth-Kelly mill stayed open only part of the time. The Commercial Bank closed in 1931 and the First National Bank folded the next year, leaving Springfield without a bank until 1940. Some workers resorted to doing farm work for 10 cents an hour. Others were lucky enough to find employment through the Civilian Conservation Corps, a federally funded program that hired young men to build trails and campgrounds in the forest.

Springfield Fire Department's truck number 4 fighting a fire in a lumber yard in the 1940s. Photo courtesy of the Springfield Museum.

Springfield's economic plight was aggravated by the forces of nature. The important hops industry met disaster in the early 1930s, when an epidemic of downey mildew infected the many hop fields in the Willamette Valley. By 1937, the mildew had decimated the industry and the hop vines were replaced with sour cherry trees.

Yet even in the darkest days of the Depression, not everything came to a standstill in Springfield. The agricultural industries did not thrive as they once had, but they continued to produce. Springfield remained a major grower of filberts through the 1930s, although the industry lost its visionary founder when George Dorris died in 1937. With the advent of large-scale irrigation systems in the 1930s, many farmers in the area began cultivating crops for canneries: corn, beets, carrots, and beans.

As farms continued to operate in the 1930s, two new granges were chartered in the Springfield area. The Mohawk-McKenzie Grange No. 747 was established in 1930, followed by the Thurston Grange No. 853 in 1936, both with grange halls. The Thurston Grange occupied

the Community Hall erected by local residents in 1913.

Springfielders still knew how to have fun during hard times. In 1937, the Playmore Theatre, a cinema, opened in Springfield, complete with Hollywood-style floodlights. An article in *The Springfield News* reported, "The large, comfortable seats were praised by many. Others liked the clear pictures on the large screen."

Outdoor entertainment could be found by fishing from a McKenzie River drift boat. Since the beginning of the century local designers had been developing highly maneuverable drift boats. From 1941 to 1960, Springfield boat builder Woodie Hindman produced boats that are typical of those used throughout the Northwest today.

In 1937 the McKenzie River Guides inaugurated a tradition of taking a run down the river one week before fishing season to note changes in the river's course and scout out good fishing holes. They often brought their wives and shared a picnic lunch. The outing took on a festive air, and friends started to join the guides. Soon the affair became so large that boats were strung out along the river, with tens of thousands of spectators applauding along the river banks. The event, known as the

McKenzie White Water Parade, occurred annually until 1970, when it was discontinued after reckless behavior led to several drownings.

By the early 1940s, the weight of the Depression began to lift and Springfielders could see the first hints of better economic times. In late 1940, the Rosboro Lumber Company, originally from Arkansas, advertised its new mill as "one of the largest and most modern sawmills in the state." Springfield Plywood, another large company, offered the generous wage of 65 cents an hour in the early 1940s, a welcome improvement over Depression-era wages.

Springfield's Armory, built on Main Street in 1921, served as headquarters for the Springfield National Guard unit that was active in the South Pacific during World War II as part of the Forty-first Division. The Armory was the scene of many lively dances, with music provided by a talented youth band.

The World War II era brought economic prosperity to the entire nation, and Springfield enjoyed a healthy boom in industry. The Booth-Kelly Mill expanded and modernized in 1948. In 1949, the Weyerhaeuser Company opened a sawmill and paper mill in Springfield,

Uniformed police officers in front of the Police Department at 240 Main Street. Photo courtesy of the Springfield Museum.

employing 800 people. Weyerhaeuser first laid roots in the Springfield area when it bought 31,000 acres of timberlands in 1907. By 1948, the company owned 155,000 acres of forest holdings.

The Springfield mill made Weyerhaeuser a leader in lumber production, and established the Willamette Valley as the timber capital of the United States. With its hordes of mill workers, Springfield came to be called the "Lunch Bucket City." Under the guidance of George Weyerhaeuser, president and CEO, the company was active in the hospital campaign in the 1950s and instrumental in achieving the East Springfield annexation in 1959.

Springfield's flax industry also was bolstered by the war. In 1939, 3,900 acres of flax were cultivated in the Springfield area. During World War II, flax was declared a defense commodity and was used to manufacture parachute harnesses, fire hose, bomb slings, linen thread for army shoes, packing material for marine engines, signal halyards, and other war items. In 1952, flax production had grown to 18,000 acres in cultivation.

The 1940s saw the development of publicly owned facilities in Springfield. By 1944, Lane County District Attorney (later Judge) William S. Fort had convinced citizens to vote in favor of a park and recreation district. The Willamalane Park and Recreation District optimistically began its first fiscal year in July 1945, without a budget or property. The name Willamalane was selected by Fort, who combined the words "Willamette" and "Lane."

Walter Hansen served as Willamalane's first superintendent, with a proposed budget of $25,000. He oversaw the District's first property purchases: Willamalane Park, acquired for $200, and James Park, purchased for a bargain $10. In the late 1940s, Willamalane received its largest funding yet. Voters approved a $285,000 bond issue for a pool and community center, and the Booth Kelly Lumber Co. provided a $25,000 gift for the development of Willamalane Park. Both the Willamalane Pool and the Veterans' War Memorial Building (a park district community center) were completed in 1951. Later in the 1950s, Willamalane expanded with the acquisition of Island Park.

City government changed when Mayor Claude Gerlach, who served from 1945-49, supported the adoption of the city manager system. Mandated by charter

(left) If all roads led to Rome, it seemed as if all logs came to Springfield's Booth-Kelly Mill. Photo courtesy of the Springfield Museum.

Christmas rush at the postal office in the IOOF Building lobby, 1947. Photo courtesy of the Springfield Museum.

amendment in 1947, the new system provided professional administration for the city. Gerlach was also responsible in part for the formation of the Central Lane Planning Organization which brought the first land use planning to the region. Its longtime director, Howard Buford, initiated the metro area's infrastructure planning.

Springfield gained a public electric and power system in 1950, after more than ten years of heated debate over publicly owned power. Springfield previously contracted for power from Mountain States Power, a private company. After two contentious elections, a charter amendment to establish a municipal utility board finally passed in 1949. On September 5, 1950, the newly formed Springfield Municipal Power initiated service to its first customers. The following month, the Springfield City Council transferred responsibility for the City of Springfield Utility Board (SUB) to an independent board of five Springfield citizens. Frank Brown was the first superintendent, followed by Jack Criswell, who served for 21 years.

By 1950, Springfield had a population of 10,087, an enormous leap from 3,805 in 1940. New schools, churches, and other community fixtures popped up throughout the area to accommodate the fast-paced growth. In 1942, Springfield High School moved into a new single-story building on 10th Street. By 1948, nearly 1,000 students were enrolled in the high school, taught by a staff of 36 teachers.

Mount Vernon was absorbed into the Springfield school district in 1948. In 1949, a new Maple Elementary School opened its doors, and Goshen and Camp Creek Elementary Schools were built. The following year was a boom year for education in Springfield, with four new schools: Walterville, Thurston, Moffitt, and Springfield Middle. The 1950s saw continued growth of the school system. Thurston Middle and Page Elementary schools opened in 1953, Hamlin Middle School was established in 1957, and Thurston High School opened in 1959.

Springfield also acquired several new churches in the 1940s. The Trinity Baptist Church opened in 1942, and North Springfield Church of Christ and Hope Lutheran were established in 1946. The Camp Creek Community Church was formed in 1943, and Twin Rivers Baptist Church in 1950.

More people also meant more movie theaters. In 1946, the McKenzie Theater held its grand opening with a screening of the film *The Virginian*. In the 1950s, Springfielders could view films from their cars at the Motor-Vu and Cascade drive-in theaters. Equally exciting was a small municipal airport, McKenzie Field, which served as home of McKenzie Flying Service. The airport was located south of Olympic Boulevard between 21 and 28 Streets.

After the Springfield General Hospital closed in 1936, the city went for nearly two decades without a hospital. As Springfield's population grew, however, Springfielders could no longer depend on the medical facilities of Eugene. In 1953, community members organized and established the Founders Service Organization, a group of 160 individuals who volunteered time and fundraising efforts to finance a hospital. Harry Wright became chair of the campaign by the flip of a coin, and then served as the hospital's first board president.

On May 1, 1955, McKenzie-Willamette Medical Services, located at 14th and G streets, opened to the Springfield community with Pete Fleissner as administrator. The next day, the hospital admitted its first patient, and the following morning, McKenzie-Willamette's first baby was born. The hospital was supported by donations from local granges, businesses, and civic organizations, as well as individuals.

While Springfield's rapid growth in the 1940s and '50s represented a strong economy, it did pose some new problems. Industry expanded along the southern edge of town, and residential areas moved north and east, away from the downtown area. This shift away from downtown, combined with the draw of a larger market area in Eugene, resulted in a decline of downtown commerce. Traffic increased on Main Street to the point that the city rerouted eastbound traffic onto South A, and in 1957 a second bridge across the Willamette was built.

Springfield held its first Christmas Parade in 1953 to denote the beginning of the holiday shopping season downtown. Even though the downtown gradually dwindled as a retail center, the annual parade was a hit. Today, as it continues to draw thousands of spectators, it is considered the "oldest and coldest" Christmas parade in Oregon.

In an attempt to revitalize the downtown area, the Springfield Chamber of Commerce sponsored a program called "Shoppers' Paradise" in 1957. The brainstorm of

Rain didn't deter the cheerleaders at Springfield High School in the 1950s. Photo courtesy of the Springfield Museum.

architect and longtime planning commissioner Don Lutes, the city closed Main Street to auto traffic to create a pedestrian mall for one week in August. The mall gained national recognition as the precursor of many downtown malls in other cities, but Springfield rejected a permanent pedestrian mall because of the difficulty of rerouting traffic.

The city also made efforts to improve Third Street, which showed signs of urban decline. With a federal grant and encouragement from Mayor Ed Harms, Springfield implemented the Third Street Urban Renewal Project from 1959 through the early 1960s. The project, which covered one-tenth of the city, demolished decaying houses and commercial buildings, paved streets, and added lights and sidewalks. A similar project along Mill Street created more through streets in 1958. Willamalane developed Meadow Park, and the city campaigned among residents for voluntary property improvement.

The 1950s decade was an idyllic time for the economy of the United States, and it was a definitive period for Springfield. The city became firmly established as a leading producer of lumber, and it flourished with new schools, publicly owned power, and a park and recreation district. The strong sense of community would help Springfield weather the storms of the 1960s and beyond. ❂

IMPORTANT DATES:

1932: Last bank in Springfield closed due to Depression.

1940s: Timber industry booming. Weyerhaeuser, Rosboro, Springfield Plywood and others opened for business.

1944: Willamalane Park & Recreation District formed.

1947: City manager system adopted.

1950: Springfield Utility Board formed.

1955: McKenzie-Willamette Hospital opened.

1958-59: Urban renewal projects.

(opposite page) Massive old-growth logs such as this one cut in 1958 are rarely seen anymore. Photo courtesy of the Springfield Museum.

(left) Mayor Edward Harms greeting the crowd at Shoppers' Paradise in 1957, during which the downtown streets were temporarily converted to pedestrian malls. Photo courtesy of the Springfield Museum.

(above) The huge Weyerhaeuser Mill under construction in 1949 in eastern Springfield. Photo courtesy of the Weyerhaeuser Company.

(opposite page) The Jay-Cees served thousands of chickens at their annual Broiler Festival, held at Willamalane Park and other locations. Photo courtesy of the Springfield Museum.

Booth Kelly Mill employees in 1946. Photo courtesy of the Springfield Museum.

Chapter Seven

TOWARD THE MILLENNIUM
1960-1999

In 1960 Springfield was still proud to be known as

Lunch Bucket City. Lumber was still king, Main Street still

had department stores (although sales were down), and giant malls

were just a glint in some far-sighted developer's eye. Their time would

come, however. Springfielders had just voted to triple the size of their

city by annexing the Thurston area, and between 1960 and 1961

the city burgeoned from 3.3 square miles to 8.61 square miles.

(above) Olympic runner, Maria Mutola of Mozambique, came to Springfield in 1991 as a teenager to train with coach Margo Jennings and the Springfield High School track team. Since graduation she has become a world-class runner, garnering numerous awards, including a bronze medal in the 1996 Olympic 800 meters. Photo courtesy of The Register-Guard. (right) Main Street in the early 1960s still featured a variety of retail businesses. Photo courtesy of the Springfield Area Chamber of Commerce.

(top) Willamalane Pool was covered with a roof in 1963 for year-round recreational swimming, classes, and swim meets. Later the Park District added a separate diving pool and a 150-foot water slide. Photo courtesy of Willamalane Park & Recreation District.

(above) Generations of Springfielders have learned to swim at Willamalane Pool. Photo courtesy of Willamalane Park & Recreation District.

*A*s the city grew, the Springfield Utility Board kept up by rapidly expanding its capacities. The agency built new substations and bought the McKenzie Highway Water District, as well as the Eugene Water & Electric Board's electrical facilities in east Springfield. Sales of electricity soared from 8.7 million kilowatt hours in 1951 to 83.4 million kilowatt hours in 1960. When the "storm of the century" struck on Columbus Day, 1962, SUB was ready. As gale force winds toppled trees and power poles, the general manager ordered all power shut off until the storm subsided. Live wires whipping throughout the city were quickly tamed. Amazingly, workers restored most power within 24 hours.*

Even though the U.S. Army Corps of Engineers began building flood control dams on the Willamette River in the 1940s, the dams overflowed during the "100-year flood" of 1964. Around Christmas over 13 inches of rain fell in seven days and hundreds of Lane County residents had to evacuate their homes. Another major flood occurred in February 1996, when the Springfield Country Club's golf course became a lake.

In spite of occasional storms, flooding, and the sudden increase in the city's size, in many ways life in Springfield at the beginning of the sixties appeared similar to the idealized suburban life portrayed on television in *Leave it to Beaver* or *Ozzie and Harriet*. Willamalane Park and Recreation District received an award as the outstanding park system in Oregon. The swimming pool at Willamalane Park was

covered with an arched roof, making swimming classes and competitive swimming possible year-round. In 1966 Kingsford Company opened, manufacturing charcoal briquettes for suburban barbecues across the country.

In 1964 Bill Dellinger, a Springfield High School graduate and 30-year-old track coach at Thurston High, won a bronze medal for the 5000-meter race at the Tokyo Olympics. The hometown hero had already performed in two previous Olympics, and would go on to become a legendary coach at the University of Oregon.

Dellinger's colleague, Bill Bowerman, who lived just outside Springfield, is credited with inspiring the jogging movement in America after a visit to New Zealand in 1962. We also know him as the amateur athletic shoe designer who was instrumental in the development of Nike, Inc. When Bowerman poured latex into his wife's waffle iron in an attempt to create a lighter shoe for the world-famous runners he coached, he changed the course of sportswear history.

At about the same time, Ken Kesey, another Springfield High graduate, was gaining praise for his literature, and notoriety for his antics. His early novels, *One Flew Over the Cuckoo's Nest* and *Sometimes a Great Notion*, are considered among the finest books of this century.

While Kesey was writing, his brother and sister-in-law, Chuck and Sue Kesey, reopened the old Springfield Creamery in 1960. In 1970 they began producing Nancy's Yogurt (now sold in 33 states), and opened their Health Food & Pool Store, thus initiating the natural

foods movement locally. By 1987 the Creamery needed so much more space that it had to move to ten acres near the Eugene Airport.

As the 1960s drew to a close, the insular attitudes of small-town life were no longer possible. By 1969 the nation was torn over the war in Vietnam, a war that intruded upon daily lives like no other previous conflict. Even the nearby University of Oregon had its share of demonstrations. President Kennedy, Senator Robert Kennedy, and Martin Luther King, Jr. had been murdered. Richard Nixon was president, and confusion and dissension spread throughout the country.

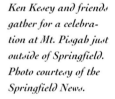

Ken Kesey and friends gather for a celebration at Mt. Pisgah just outside of Springfield. Photo courtesy of the Springfield News.

Springfielder Bill Dellinger has spent a lifetime at tracks, both running and coaching. He won a bronze medal for the 5000-meter race at the Tokyo Olympics in 1964. Photo courtesy of the University of Oregon Athletic Department.

Local news was often far more encouraging than national and international news. In 1972 the generosity of the Dorris family allowed Willamalane to purchase the beautiful Dorris Ranch, the first filbert raising operation in the country. The historic ranch, a prime riverfront property, would be preserved for the enjoyment of future generations.

Although several local banks opened and closed after the Depression, Centennial Bank opened in 1974 and continued to grow with the community. The mid-seventies were hard years for downtown businesses, however. With the growth of regional shopping malls, notably Valley River Center in Eugene and the smaller Springfield Mall built in 1975, downtown Springfield lost Woolworth, Emporium, and other retail businesses. As in many other small cities, Main Street was no longer the primary shopping area.

Not far from downtown, Willamalane built its Senior Adult Activity Center at Island Park in 1979. The attractive 22,000-square-foot facility, designed by local architects Lutes & Sanatel, is one of the largest senior centers in the Northwest. Programs are extensive, and the Senior Center has been enormously successful since its inauguration.

While the Senior Center prospered, a major downtown business was floundering. An elevated shopping center, Spring Village, needed a bailout, and Springfield urgently needed a new city hall, having outgrown its modest facility on A Street. City Councilor Don Carter presented the idea of remodeling Spring Village into a combined city hall and library complex, at a much lower cost than constructing from scratch. The idea caught on with the thrifty administration and equally thrifty citizens. The architects Lutes & Sanatel were called in, and they successfully transformed Spring Village into an $8-million modern administrative center.

Adjacent to City Hall was the former Pacific Power & Light Company headquarters on Main Street. The city's Historical Commission acted quickly to secure the dis-

tinctive 1911 building as a historic museum. The museum opened in 1981, with temporary displays reflecting the history of Springfield. Later a permanent interpretive center was installed upstairs.

In 1982 Springfield gained its first television station when KMTR-TV opened as Eugene-Springfield's new all-NBC affiliate. The company was founded by mostly local shareholders, and launched additional stations in Coos Bay and Roseburg in 1991 and 1992.

With the continued growth of Springfield's population, McKenzie-Willamette Hospital, like City Hall, was bursting at the seams by 1980. In 1983 it opened its $16.5 million ancillary building, and in 1989 it became the first hospital in the state to receive Level II Trauma Care status. In 1999 McKenzie-Willamette operated the only adult day health care center in the region, and its Occupational Health Program served 1500 regional businesses.

From 1979 to 1983, even though Springfield gained a new City Hall and library, a TV station, a museum, and a greatly enlarged hospital, the local economy suffered from the same recession that struck the entire nation. With construction faltering, mill towns like Springfield experienced extensive layoffs. The passage of the Endangered Species Act in 1973 led to changes in logging practices that dealt a blow to the lumber industry both locally and nationally. For a time, the endangered spotted owl symbolized a deep rift in local sentiment.

During the recession, some residents left the area, looking for opportunities in Alaska and elsewhere. Even after the economy improved, lumber companies continued to face difficulties. Springfield's major mill, Weyerhaeuser, had to close one of its operations, the plywood plant, in 1985. That same year Georgia-Pacific mitigated some of its problems by donating the old Booth-Kelly mill site to the City. Known as the Big M Shopping Center for a few years, the historic buildings now house a number of start-up manufacturing businesses.

1985 was a happy year for history buffs. Springfielders celebrated the city's centennial with ongoing activities, including the production of an original history play, *Springfield Visits the World*, by D. Velasco. As a result of the Centennial Celebrations, Springfield formed an Arts Commission in 1986, and created the Centennial Fountain outside City Hall in 1988. Ceramic artist Alan Kluber designed and installed colorful tile work around the fountain's rim.

Springfield's Historical Commission, in recognition of the centennial, had been working to gain a listing on the National Register of Historic Places for its historic residential area, the Washburne District. Approved in 1985, this historical designation of an entire working-class neighborhood was highly unusual. The district encompasses most of the city's old grid-style blocks platted between 1872 and 1890, including 29 entire blocks and five partial blocks. Nearly 44 percent of the houses were built between 1890 and 1915, while 23 percent were built between 1915 and 1930. Most of the houses were constructed of Douglas fir, the predominant timber in the area. Typical styles are the Mill Cottage, Homestead House, Transitional Box, and Bungalow.

In 1986 Willamalane received the National Gold Medal Award for excellence in park and recreation management. The next year it again gained attention by opening Dorris Ranch to the public as Oregon's first living history farm. In 1988 Dorris Ranch received its designation on the National Register of Historic Places. And, when Willamalane built the Lively Park Swim Center in 1989 (named for Jack B. Lively, longtime supporter and donor), it was the Northwest's first indoor wave-action pool.

Art and history often intermingled in Springfield. Beginning in 1987 the Arts Commission hired numerous artists to create murals and other public art on a modest scale. Murals were painted along Art Alley, covering topics as wide-ranging as traditional scenes by Ann Woodruff Murray, the whimsical Bob the Dog by John Swenson, and cool, abstracted shapes by Alan Cox.

Woodruff Murray created her masterpiece, the Oregon Trail mural located on the east side of the historic Gerlach building, from 1993-94. The 120-foot long mural honors the Oregon Trail Sesquicentennial. Eugene artist Jerry Williams installed his whimsical rhino sculpture outside the library in 1994, and Springfield's annual Puppet Festival has been delighting children and adults alike since 1993. Emerald Empire Art Association, which owns a large downtown gallery and offers art classes, has been active since 1959.

In 1989 the historic railroad depot was moved from its original site to the city's western entry. A major restora-

(below) Youngsters ham it up on a float in the annual Christmas Parade, held each year since 1953. Photo courtesy of the Springfield News.

Hall of Famer Bobby Doerr, who played with the Boston Red Socks, helped develop the pee-wee baseball clinics at Willamalane Park & Recreation District. Doerr still lives in the area. Photo courtesy of Willamalane Park & Recreation District.

(right) Bill Morrisette served as mayor for 10 years until 1998, when he became a state representative. Photo courtesy of the Springfield News.

tion project was undertaken as a grass roots effort, and the Stick Chalet-style building, which is the only depot of its kind still standing in Oregon, now houses the Springfield Chamber of Commerce and a visitor center for the city.

While the depot is a vivid reminder of Springfield's history, a whole new retail and business cluster has developed at the Gateway area adjacent to the I-5 freeway. The neon-decorated Gateway Mall, opened in 1990, is a major attraction. In 1994 Sony Disc Manufacturing began operation in a beautiful campus setting near the McKenzie River. In 1999 Sony employed 400 workers to produce 12 million audio CD, CD-ROM, and PlayStation discs per month.

Among other Gateway businesses are Shorewood Packaging and Cascade Fabrication. In 1999 ground was broken for a new city sports complex. Because of rapid development and heavy traffic in the Gateway area, plans at the end of the century were underway for a new freeway interchange.

To help workers prepare for new jobs in Gateway and other business developments, Lane Community College, located in southeast Eugene, opened an off-campus learning center in Springfield in 1997. That same year three new schools opened, including Agnes Stewart Middle School, named for Springfield's first teacher. In 1999 Springfield had a public school student population of 12,000 in 16 elementary schools, five middle schools, and two high schools.

When children who were first graders in 1999 graduate from high school, Springfield will be considerably

changed. The population is expected to grow to 85,000 by 2015, and that population will become increasingly diverse as more Latinos and other minorities move to Springfield. Local factories may be manufacturing products not yet invented. High school and university graduates will have job titles not yet imagined. Springfield will probably have a new civic center, a new library, and more sports complexes.

All indications point toward Springfield continuing to be a place where hard workers can make a good life for their families. Like Elias and Mary Briggs, and the Kalapuya Indians before them, Springfielders in the new millennium will still enjoy the beauty of the rivers and the bounty of the land. ✿

IMPORTANT DATES:

1960-61:	Thurston and other areas annexed.
1972:	Dorris Ranch purchased by Willamalane.
1975-79:	Springfielder Robert Straub Governor of Oregon.
1979-81:	Senior Center, new City Hall and Springfield Museum opened.
1985:	Springfield Centennial celebrated.
1990:	Gateway Mall opened.

Epilogue

At the end of the twentieth century, many favorable changes are within sight on Springfield's horizon. A part of Glenwood, traditionally known as West Springfield, was annexed to the city in 1999, strengthening its historic ties to the city. A non-profit organization, Springfield Renaissance Development Corporation, is building upon the efforts of earlier civic improvement groups to bring the focus of future development back to the historic heart of the city at the Willamette River.

Springfielders haven't always been in perfect agreement, however. Throughout the years, Springfield has weathered its fair share of conflicts, tragedies, and political mistakes. Highly publicized cases of discrimination and violence have attracted national attention. Nevertheless, Springfield is not unique in its problems, which are similar to those found throughout the United States.

What has been admirable is Springfield's determination to maintain its essential cohesion and enhance its sense of community. When the Booth-Kelly Mill burned back in 1911, Springfield's entire economy was devastated. It wasn't the first time a major mill had burned, however, and Springfielders have always chosen to stay and rebuild, whether the problem was a burnt mill, a washed-out bridge, or a social conflict.

Each generation tries to make a better city and a better life for the next generation. In Springfield we are fortunate that our individual voices are loud enough to be heard. Every community member can participate in Springfield's government at some level. Springfield's mayors and councilors have been ordinary men and women—blacksmiths, small business owners, bus drivers, and school teachers. Anyone who has an interest can be a part of the decision making.

The desire of Springfielders to provide family recreation, social support, and public safety, to preserve our history, and to retain a modest, accessible government structure is evidence of Springfield's enduring pioneer spirit. Springfield has been blessed with rich natural resources and a glorious setting, but it is the resilience, determination, and ingenuity of generations of Springfielders that has given the community its abiding strength.

SPRINGFIELD TODAY

The Springfield Depot now houses the Springfield Area Chamber of Commerce office and serves as an Oregon Tourist Information Center. The historic train car is permanently stationed at the loading dock. Photo courtesy of the Springfield Area Chamber of Commerce.

Sony Disc Manufacturing was a welcome addition to the Gateway area, and to the labor market of the entire metropolitan area, when it opened in 1994. Photo courtesy of Sony Disc Manufacturing.

(top, left) Haunted Halloween is a popular event at the Dorris Ranch. Photo courtesy of Willamalane Park & Recreation District.

(bottom, left) Agnes Stewart Middle School, opened in 1997, honors Springfield's first teacher. Photo courtesy of Camdon Draeger, Moderne Studios.

(top, right) Anne Woodruff Murray's colorful Oregon Trail mural is admired by residents and visitors alike. Photo courtesy of Camdon Draeger, Moderne Studios.

(bottom, right) University of Oregon students designed this statue of a Native American on a horse, causing several decades of debate over its artistic merit. The statue is located at Springfield's western entrance. Photo courtesy of Camdon Draeger, Moderne Studios.

The Native American camp is an important feature of the Filbert Festival, held each August at Island Park. Photo courtesy of the Springfield News.

The Lively Park Swim Center houses the Northwest's first indoor wave pool, a six-lane, 25-yard lap pool, a 26-person Jacuzzi, a family swim area, a 136-foot water slide, and a kiddie pool. Photo courtesy of Willamalane Park & Recreation District.

Pesky squirrels love hazelnuts and play a large role in crop loss at the Dorris Ranch. The ranch hires live trappers to relocate them on BLM lands. Photo courtesy of Willamalane Park & Recreation District.

The cast of Whistle Stops, an original musical about the coming of the railroads to the Northwest, poses at the Springfield Depot before it was moved and renovated. Photo courtesy of Sparky J. Roberts.

(bottom, left) Island Park is a center of recreation and special events in Springfield. Photo courtesy of Willamalane Park & Recreation District.

(bottom, right) Main sitting room of the Willamalane Senior Adult Activity Center, built in 1979 at Island Park. Photo courtesy of Willamalane Park & Recreation District.

Chapter Eight

Partners in Progress

FOUNDING TO 1925

Laying the cornerstone of the IOOF building was an important event involving men, women and children in all their finery.
Photo courtesy of the Springfield Museum.

WEYERHAEUSER

Weyerhaeuser's second paper machine, installed in 1965, tripled the mill's production of linerboard, the smooth inner and outer lining of corrugated cartons. Photo by Robert Lindsay & Associates.

At peak production in the late 1980s, the sawmill manufactured 120 million board feet of lumber annually, enough to build 10,000 average-sized homes every year.

To make full use of the wood resource, Weyerhaeuser pioneered an integrated manufacturing strategy in Springfield. A common practice at the time was to burn sawmill wood residuals in cone-shaped "wigwams." Instead, Weyerhaeuser's new paper mill was designed to use sawmill residuals to make paper—known as "linerboard" or "containerboard"—for corrugated cartons. The Springfield operations even used tree bark to generate steam for manufacturing and power.

Springfield's beautiful urban trees change with the seasons and thrive over the decades, living symbols of change and longevity.

The history of Weyerhaeuser in Springfield is also a story of change and longevity. For the past 50 years, Weyerhaeuser's Springfield operations have employed thousands of people, manufactured world-class products, and set high environmental standards. The company has appreciated the long-time support of Springfield residents and local businesses.

Weyerhaeuser's story reflects the ingenuity and dedication of its employees, and the successful partnerships with the Association of Western Pulp and Paper Workers (AWPPW), the current International Association of Machinists and Aerospace Workers (IAM&AW), and the former International Woodworkers Association (IWA).

Weyerhaeuser established its roots in the Springfield area in 1907, when the company made its first timberlands purchase of 31,000 acres. By 1940, the company had increased its forestland holdings to 58,000 acres, and in 1948, Weyerhaeuser founded the 155,000-acre Calapooya Tree Farm. Today, Weyerhaeuser owns about 400,000 acres in the southern Willamette valley.

Over the years, Weyerhaeuser's Springfield facilities have produced lumber, plywood, ply-veneer, particleboard, presto-logs, and paper. Weyerhaeuser has also supplied many other mills in the area with logs and chips.

During the 1940s, the company turned pasture land east of Springfield into a 450-acre plant site, and in 1949, opened a sawmill and a paper mill employing 800 people. The sawmill produced premium-quality, Douglas-fir lumber, initially producing 250,000 board feet per day.

The paper mill, Springfield Containerboard, is testimony to 50 years of hard work, innovation, and strategic investment. Originally designed to produce 150 tons of linerboard per day on one paper machine, it reached 250 tons per day by 1951. In 1965, the company added a second paper machine, boosting production to 900 tons per day. Today, the plant's capacity is nearly 2,000 tons daily, totaling 690,000 tons per year.

The company's Springfield plant site expanded from lumber and containerboard into other areas of wood products manufacturing during the past half century. From 1950 until the late 1980s, the presto-log operation produced eight-pound fuel logs from planer shavings. The plywood plant, which operated for 33 years beginning in 1952, produced 170,000 square-feet of veneer per day, making it one of the largest plywood facilities in the Pacific Northwest.

Also on its Springfield plant site, Weyerhaeuser opened a ply-veneer plant in 1952 which produced paper-overlayed veneer to make sturdy containers for the agricultural industry. The annual production is 25 million square feet per year. Weyerhaeuser began operating a particleboard facility in 1969 using wood residuals—sawdust and shavings—to produce engineered panel products. The product is primarily used in countertops,

The Springfield sawmill produced fine-grained, clear Douglas-fir lumber from large logs during 1949 to 1991. In 1988, the mill produced custom-sized lumber for restoration of the USS Constellation.

cabinetry, and furniture components. Annual particleboard capacity is 180 million square feet (3/4-inch basis). Both of these operations were sold to SierraPine Ltd. in May, 1999.

In 1974, Springfield Containerboard began recycling pre-consumer wastepaper to make the manufacturing process more cost-efficient and environmentally friendly. In 1993, the company invested $70 million to begin recycling post-consumer OCC (old corrugated containers). Today, the Springfield paper plant manufactures paper with more than 30 percent recycled content, using up to 800 tons of wastepaper per day. This amount is equivalent to the box waste from 400 large supermarkets. Since 1974, Weyerhaeuser Company has become one of the largest paper recycling operations in North America.

Just as Springfield's urban trees have endured trying times over the decades, so Weyerhaeuser has faced difficult conditions. In recent years, higher log costs combined with a reduced supply of federal timber and challenging global market conditions have adversely impacted the forest products industry. Faced with these conditions, Weyerhaeuser closed its Springfield plywood plant in 1985 and its large-log sawmill in 1991.

The company continues to produce containerboard at its Springfield plant site. Other local Weyerhaeuser facilities include a recycling center, hardwood sawmill and wood products distribution center in Eugene, a small-log sawmill in Cottage Grove, and timberlands operation offices in Springfield and Cottage Grove.

Community Involvement

The company and Weyerhaeuser people have long supported the community through volunteerism and philanthropy. The Weyerhaeuser Company Foundation has provided more than $2 million over the past 20 years to local nonprofit organizations. For many years, donations by Weyerhaeuser employees and grants from the company's Foundation have represented the largest annual contribution to United Way of Lane County. Company employees are actively involved in the community, helping children learn to read, cleaning up parks, serving on civic groups, and participating in many other ways.

Weyerhaeuser's contribution to Springfield residents as an employer and taxpayer is significant. The company currently employs more than 650 employees in Springfield, with an annual payroll of nearly $35 million. Annual property taxes to the local Springfield economy are nearly $7 million. In addition, the company spends about $85 million every year on local goods and services.

Environmental Care

Weyerhaeuser's vision is to be the best forest products company in the world. Achieving this vision includes maintaining a healthy balance between meeting the demand for wood products and protecting the environment.

Weyerhaeuser's Springfield manufacturing facilities have set high standards for environmental protection for the past 50 years. Weyerhaeuser's principles of "reduce, reuse and recycle" guide its facilities in minimizing the environmental impact of operations. Operations are rigorously monitored and controlled to ensure all local, state, and federal environmental requirements are met or exceeded. Since 1970, Weyerhaeuser has continually invested in technological improvements to expand and modernize its facilities and improve environmental quality.

The white plumes coming from the Springfield Containerboard stacks are 99 percent steam, generated from the paper making process. The remainder are combustion by-products, which are regulated under state and federal air permits. One element of emissions is particulate matter (PM), the same material emitted by wood stoves. Since 1978, Springfield facilities have reduced PM emissions by 65 percent to levels well below permitted limits.

Bales of used office paper are processed without bleaching into new linerboard at Springfield Containerboard. The mill began using recycled paper in 1974. In 1993, the company invested $70 million to recycle old corrugated cartons as another source of used paper.

Springfield Containerboard uses state-of-the-art water treatment processes to protect the McKenzie River, the mill's source of water. Water is cooled to river temperature in the company's cooling ponds (shown here) before returning to the river. The ponds provide habitat for fish, waterfowl, and other wildlife.

The paper mill also emits small amounts of gases that have a "rotten egg" odor. Since 1975, the mill has reduced these emissions by 80 percent, achieving one of the lowest levels in the paper industry. The mill's goal is to completely eliminate odor, but the necessary technology does not yet exist.

The Springfield paper mill currently uses less than one percent of the McKenzie River's daily flow in its pulp and paper process. Nearly half of the water is used to cool manufacturing equipment. This water passes through cooling ponds before returning to the river. Water used in the paper making process is reused many times, then treated before being returned safely to the McKenzie River. The company carefully monitors water quality in conjunction with regulatory agencies to ensure compliance with applicable regulations. Weyerhaeuser is fully committed to protecting the quality of the McKenzie River.

We have also improved our stormwater management practices, enhanced fish and wildlife habitat within our plant site, and increased the recycling of various materials including batteries, fluorescent light tubes, and asphalt. We are working with state agencies to study groundwater conditions at our Springfield plant site, and developing management plans to ensure that public water resources remain protected.

Sustainable Forestry

When Frederick Weyerhaeuser and 15 partners founded Weyerhaeuser Company in 1900, Frederick stated that renewable forestry, " . . . is not for us, nor for our children, but for our grandchildren." The long-term philosophy embodied in his statement has remained the foundation of Weyerhaeuser's approach to forest management.

Mr. Weyerhaeuser believed that forestland was a valuable long-term asset which must be managed for the future. Weyerhaeuser's forestland purchases in the Willamette area during the first half of the 1900s provided the raw material base for sustained manufacturing operations in Springfield.

In 1941, Weyerhaeuser dedicated the nation's first certified tree farm, launching an American Tree Farm

System that now includes nearly 90 million acres of private forestland across all 50 states. In 1966, the company began its High Yield Forestry Program to improve the quality and volume of wood in its forests. This program includes developing genetically improved seedlings, continuous replanting to replace harvested trees, nurturing tree growth through thinning and fertilizing, and protecting the young trees from fire, insects, and disease.

Weyerhaeuser replants usually within one year after harvest, currently planting 400 to 600 seedlings per acre. Since the 1950s, the company has planted more than 125 million trees in the Willamette area, 315 million in Oregon, and 2.5 billion trees across the nation. The company participates in the Sustainable Forest Initiative™ sponsored by the American Forest & Paper Association, and manages two million acres of west-side forestland in Oregon and Washington in compliance with the initiative.

Weyerhaeuser bases its forest practices on sound, state-of-the-art science. The company's forestry research organization has received worldwide recognition for its work in silvicultural and environmental sciences. Through technological progress and environmental foresight, Weyerhaeuser now produces twice as much lumber, paper, fiber, and other wood products from an acre of forest.

For Weyerhaeuser, responsible forest management means more than growing productive forests. It also means protecting fish and wildlife habitat and other benefits of our natural heritage. Company foresters and scientists are finding better ways to keep streams healthy for fish, and to provide diverse wildlife habitat across the forest landscape. The centerpiece of the company's forest practices is its watershed analysis program. The program

assesses watershed conditions and identifies resource sensitivities. This information enables managers and other watershed stakeholders, including landowners and agencies, to develop site-specific prescriptions that guide forest management activities while protecting water quality and fish habitat.

Being the best forest products company in the world means focusing on the future while managing change. Weyerhaeuser's efforts to care for the forest environment—as well as the trees—will sustain vital natural resources and ensure a supply of raw materials for its Lane County facilities for generations to come. ●

Weyerhaeuser began operating the Mohawk Valley railroad in 1961 to transport logs from the company's sort yard along the Mohawk River to the Springfield sawmill, a trip of 22 miles. Affectionately called the "Mohawk Rocket," the train operated until 1989.

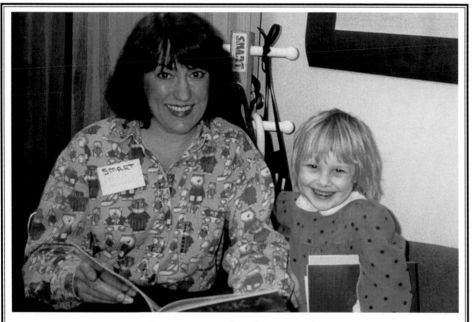

Supporting the Community
Local Groups in Springfield supported by Weyerhaeuser

- Kidsports
- Local schools
- Oregon Trail Boy Scouts
- SMART (Start Making a Reader Today)
- Salmon Watch
- Springfield Filbert Festival
- Springfield Museum
- Springfield Community Band
- Springfield Chamber of Commerce
- United Way of Lane County
- United Way YouthWorks
- Western Rivers Girl Scouts
- Willamalane Parks and Recreation District
- Many other local nonprofit organizations

Weyerhaeuser employees support many local organizations and volunteer for many civic programs. Here, an employee helps a kindergarten student learn to read as part of the SMART program.

CITY OF SPRINGFIELD

The first evidence of an organized Springfield community came less than eight years after the arrival of pioneers Elias and Mary Briggs. A townsite plat was filed on December 24, 1856, encompassing a two-block area between South A and Main Streets and Mill and Third Streets.

The City of Springfield was incorporated on February 25, 1885. Albert Walker, a local blacksmith, was elected the first mayor. By the turn of the century, city government consisted of a mayor, four city councilmen, a recorder, and a treasurer. The only staff position was that of Town Marshal, who was paid a salary of $10 per month in 1900.

Fire protection was provided through a volunteer fire company, organized in 1886.

Other than keeping the peace and protecting property, the most important activities in those early years were public works projects, and the most significant of these was the paving of Main Street.

In 1911, the City Council passed an ordinance to improve Main Street from Mill to 10th Streets. Like other public works projects, this work was carried out by a city-sponsored organization called "Permanent Improvement," supervised by the City Engineer.

In the 113 years since its incorporation, Springfield has grown from an area of .38 square miles to its present size of 13.5 square miles. The population, which was 390 in 1890, now stands at more than 51,000.

A growth in both the scope and size of municipal services has paralleled this increase in population and land area. The City now has a workforce of 364 full-time employees and an operating budget of $43.67 million.

It provides a full range of services, including Public Works, Planning and Development, Fire and Life Safety, Police, court services, and a Library, backed up by the Administration, Human Resources, Information Services, and Finance departments.

The City of Springfield takes pride in efficient operation and meeting challenges with optimism and creativity.

In the first decade of the century, Springfield gained a reputation for efficiency in government by operating its public improvements under city supervision, rather than through private contractors. In the early 1980s, city leaders met the need for more space and consolidated service by purchasing a failed shopping mall as the new City Hall. This placed all city services except police and maintenance under one roof.

A decade later, local leaders attacked the economic recession caused by the decline of the timber industry by making an active effort to diversify the economy. The effort has been successful and Springfield now has several high-tech corporations providing hundreds of jobs for local citizens.

Springfield will enjoy a bright future. The Springfield-Eugene area is a very desirable location to work and play.

Because of the physical beauty and the robust economy, continued growth will occur. Our challenge will be to accommodate quality growth while preserving both our rich heritage and quality of life. We can do this—we always have. ❶

SPRINGFIELD SCHOOL DISTRICT

More than 150 years ago, the Springfield School District began with the organization of the first school at Upper Camp Creek (then District No. 5) in 1848, following Eugene District No. 4 and Pleasant Hill District No. 1.

By 1854, the Oregon Territorial Government declared a "system of common schools," and Springfield School District No. 19 was officially founded.

Mrs. Agnes Stewart Warner, who had been a member of the famous "Lost Wagon Train of 1853," was hired by the newly formed district's directors—Mr. Brattain, Mr. Briggs, and Mr. Maris—to teach in Springfield's first elementary school, believed to have been at Seventh and B Streets.

Due to increasing population, another one-story, two-room school was built on Mill Street, between D and E Streets, in 1888.

Three schools have since been built on the Mill Street site. About 1889, the first building was sawed into two parts and moved east on D Street to be used as homes for many years. The second school built at the same location was a two-story, two-room school, which served about 70 students. Due to overcrowding, a few years later students in the lower grades were transferred to the site of a cheese factory, two blocks south on Mill Street.

Around 1910, Lincoln School was built as a grade school, and additions were made to the two-story building on Mill Street, which was being used as a high school. In 1921, the first high school was torn down and replaced with a new building (which would later serve as Springfield Junior High and then the Administration Building).

By 1926, the district had two elementary schools (Brattain and Lincoln) and one high school employing 31 teachers (7 men and 24 women) and educating 772 students (350 boys and 422 girls).

Maple School (not consolidated as part of the district until July 1, 1949) was organized in 1895 and labeled "Mud College." It sat on Main Street (where the Rosboro Lumber Company is today) and stood on stilts with an elevated walkway into the school from a dirt road. Another early school, Mount Vernon (District 18, pictured above, left), was consolidated with Springfield on December 4, 1945.

Many other schools first associated with District 19—such as Stafford, Cedar Flats, Leaburg, Davis, Deerhorn, Donna, Hayden Bridge, Rocky Point, and Glenwood—are no longer in existence.

For the next three decades, the population of Springfield swelled, as did the school district.

A new Springfield High School was built on 10th Street in 1941-42. It was rebuilt facing Seventh Street in 1971. Thurston High School was built in 1959.

Through its first 150 years, District 19 has evolved from wood stoves and slates, to state-of-the-art security systems and computers in every classroom.

In 1997, Springfield School District's new Agnes Stewart Middle School opened its doors to more than 600 sixth-, seventh- and eighth-grade students. Many of the present-day pioneers had no idea they were entering a school named after Springfield's first teacher, Agnes Stewart Warner.

That same year, the new Mount Vernon Elementary School (pictured above, right) opened as the first school in Lane County implementing a uniform policy, and Riverbend Elementary was added to the district's cadre.

Today, under the leadership of Jamon Kent and board members Alan Petersen, Jennifer Heiss, Marty Lenk, Fred McDaniel, and Tom Atkinson, District 19 serves more than 11,000 students in two high schools (Springfield and Thurston), five middle schools (Hamlin, Briggs, Thurston, Springfield, and Agnes Stewart), 16 elementary schools (Brattain, Maple, Goshen, Camp Creek, Walterville, Thurston, Moffitt, Elizabeth Page, Guy Lee, Yolanda, Mohawk, Douglas Gardens, Centennial, Ridgeview, Mount Vernon, and Riverbend), as well as numerous alternative education programs (such as Gateways Learning Center, Walterville and Goshen alternative programs, and the Isaac Newton Technology Program at Springfield Middle School).

In addition, the Lane Community College Learning Center was opened in December 1997, bridging education between high school and college, as well as offering educational opportunities to members of the public.

Always looking to the future, the Springfield School District continues to care about its community and its children as a district in the heart of the valley, with the valley at heart. ◑

LANE COUNTY

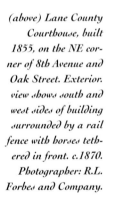

(above) Lane County Courthouse, built 1855, on the NE corner of 8th Avenue and Oak Street. Exterior view shows south and west sides of building surrounded by a rail fence with horses tethered in front. c.1870. Photographer: R.L. Forbes and Company.

Lane County Courthouse, built 1898, on the corner of 8th Avenue and Oak Street. Exterior. View from intersection showing entrance, clock tower, west and south sides of building. Horse and a carriage can be seen to the left. c.1905.

Hardy pioneers traveling the Oregon Trail in the late 1840s settled in what today is Lane County. They came here primarily to farm the Willamette Valley's fertile soil.

Originally, Lane County covered all of southern Oregon east to the Rocky Mountains and south to the California border.

It's still big today, covering 4,620 square miles from the Pacific Ocean to the Cascade Mountains. It is larger than Delaware and Rhode Island combined and is almost the size of Connecticut.

Although 90 percent of Lane County is forestland, Eugene and Springfield comprise the second largest urban area in Oregon after Portland.

The Territorial Legislature created Lane County on Jan. 29, 1851, three years after Oregon became a United States territory. It was named for General Joseph Lane, a rugged frontiersman who was Oregon's first territorial governor.

In 1852, the county's first district court met under a large oak tree until a small board shanty could be built as a clerk's office.

Many buildings served county government through the years. The first courthouse was built in 1855 at Eighth and Oak Streets. The $8,500 building was two stories high and offered offices and a courtroom.

Years later it was moved a block away and used as a high school. The second courthouse, complete with a huge brick clock tower, was built in 1898. It cost just under $50,000.

The structure was demolished in 1959 to make way for the current building, which cost $2.1 million.

Lane County's timber market opened in the 1880s as railroads arrived in the area.

Historically, Lane County's economy has been based on timber and agriculture. The area's timber industry grew rapidly because Lane County is on the edge of Oregon's largest timber stand. The Willamette Valley's fertile soil and moderate climate make it one of the nation's most productive farming areas.

Today, services, manufacturing, high technology, tourism, publishing, and trade assume a larger role in Lane County's economy. Wood products remain a large employer although harvests have diminished significantly.

Lane County government originally consisted of a county judge, three commissioners, an assessor, treasurer, and sheriff, whose job included enforcing the law and collecting taxes. A county clerk and school superintendent were added later.

In the beginning, Oregon counties were considered agents of state government. In 1963, Lane County became a home rule county, which allowed the government to make its own laws within certain state limits.

By then, only three county commissioners, an assessor, and sheriff remained. All other elected positions were abolished.

In 1969, the county enlarged its board of commissioners to five members.

Today, Lane County government performs property assessments and record keeping, road maintenance, elections, and public safety.

County employees also are involved in child and family wellness programs, economic development, employment and job training, planning and zoning, water quality, public health, and youth services.

Lane County currently is Oregon's fourth most populous county with 313,000 residents. ❶

THE SPRINGFIELD NEWS

Originally named The Nonpariel, *The Springfield News* was first published by John Wood in 1896. The name changed to *The Springfield News* in 1903 and remained under local ownership for seven decades.

Glenn Jackson of Albany became *The Springfield News's* first out-of-town owner when he purchased the newspaper in the late 1970s. Jackson also owned the Albany Democrat-Herald at the time.

The Springfield News has changed owners several times since then. Its current owner, Lee Enterprises Inc., based in Davenport, Iowa, purchased the newspaper in September 1997.

Today, *The Springfield News* employs 41 workers along with more than 100 adult and youth delivery carriers and operates a bustling printing business in addition to publishing a twice-weekly newspaper with a circulation of 10,700.

The newspaper office was located downtown for many years before moving to its current site on Laura Street in west Springfield.

Organizations such as the Oregon Newspaper Publishers Association and the Society of Professional Journalists have recognized *The Springfield News* and its staff for excellence regularly over the years.

The Oregon Newspaper Publishers Association has named *The Springfield News* Oregon's best nondaily newspaper in 1996 and 1997.

Numerous former *Springfield News* reporters and photographers have moved on to national publications.

A community newspaper that was born around the turn of the twentieth century looks toward the twenty-first century with its roots firmly planted in the community.

The newspaper has never forgotten its responsibility to serve Springfield and east Lane County and remains committed to serving the community in the future. ❂

MYRMO & SONS, INC.

George Myrmo and his wife, Olga, brought a truckload of blacksmith's tools and their three children, Helga, Arthur, and Emil, to Eugene from Glendale, Oregon in 1925.

Myrmo opened his shop, named simply George Myrmo; Blacksmith on a small lot along Franklin Boulevard.

He made heavy logging equipment, while Olga occasionally helped in the office.

Myrmo began adding machinery in the early 1930s as his shop and the business expanded.

Arthur Myrmo began working for his father in 1935, and two years later the company began building logging trailers.

The firm was renamed George Myrmo & Sons in 1938, when Emil joined his father and brother in the company.

Business was brisk during World War II as the company sold logging trailers, expanded the parts department, and repaired logging and sawmill equipment.

Myrmo bought adjacent land during the 1930s and 1940s. By the end of the war, the plant had tripled in size.

George retired after the war and his sons took over the business. In 1952, another building was added to house offices and the expanded parts department.

The company hit a milestone in 1969 when it moved to a new custom-built plant on a five-acre site in Glenwood and changed to its current name, Myrmo & Sons, Inc. The name

change recognized the arrival of a third generation into the business, when Arthur's son, George joined the company.

By 1975, when the firm celebrated its 50th anniversary, Myrmo's was about to expand again.

The company opened a Bend branch in 1977 to sell heavy-duty truck and industrial parts. It expanded in 1982 to include repair work.

In 1998, the Bend site became a Freightliner dealer. The company also opened a second Bend facility that repairs hydraulic systems and parts and serves as a machine shop.

George Myrmo, Erik Myrmo, and Craig Myrmo are involved in the company today. Fourth generation Myrmos are working part-time in the business.

Today, Emil Myrmo is retired. Arthur passed away in 1991. But, the family tradition that has guided the tiny blacksmith shop into a multimillion-dollar corporation lives on. ❂

TIMBER PRODUCTS COMPANY

A bountiful supply of Douglas fir shop lumber brought Timber Products Company's founders to Springfield in 1948. Springfield's livability and a progressive local business community have combined to keep them ever since.

Company founder J.H. "Henry" Gonyea and his son, W.H. "Wil" Gonyea, opened a door plant known as

Clear Fir Products at 1116 S. A Street in 1948. When Larry Moore joined the company in 1951, it employed a dozen people in the sales office and 75 at the door plant.

In November 1968, the company moved up the hill to its current home at 305 S. Fourth Street Timber Products Company purchased the original Booth-Kelly building from Georgia Pacific Corp. Booth-Kelly was one of Springfield's first sawmills.

Timber Products Company sold the door plant in 1973 and has not been involved in manufacturing locally since. The Springfield office now houses the administrative headquarters for a company that employs more than 1,450 workers at facilities in four states. Roughly 85 workers, including timber brokers, work in Springfield.

Timber Products Company makes softwood veneer, particleboard, plywood, and laminates at production facilities in southern Oregon, northern California, Michigan, and Mississippi. The company runs a nation-wide trucking service based in Central Point and Memphis, Tennessee, with a fleet of 130 trucks and owns 130,000 acres of timber land in northern California.

Company president J.H. Gonyea II runs the business his grandfather started. Two of his sons, J.H. Gonyea III and David Gonyea, also are active in the business. ❡

WASHINGTON MUTUAL AND WESTERN BANK

Washington Mutual and Western Bank take pride in their Northwest roots.

In 1889, Washington Mutual was founded with the goal of helping families build and purchase homes in the Northwest. Western Bank, established in 1904 as the Bank of Bandon, shares an equally rich local history.

Both banks achieved milestones and faced challenges. On February 10, 1890, Washington Mutual issued the first monthly installment home loan on the West Coast.

In 1914, the Bank of Bandon faced closure after a fire hit the business district. The directors persevered and, according to historian Curt Beckham, "after two weeks, deposits exceeded expectations and withdrawals were small."

In 1959, the Bank of Bandon changed its name to Western Bank and later, during the 1960s, the company moved its headquarters to Coos Bay. In 1974, Washington Mutual pioneered The Exchange, the first shared network of cash machines in the nation.

Washington Mutual continued in that pioneering spirit, and, in 1983, launched a growth strategy that would result in 24 successful acquisitions within 15 years.

Part of that growth strategy was the joining of Washington Mutual and Western Bank—a union that created a bank that

could better serve the needs of Oregonians.

Combined, Western Bank and Washington Mutual focus on providing premier customer service to families, individuals, and small-to mid-sized businesses.

As a bank dedicated to meeting the needs of people and smaller businesses, Washington Mutual and Western Bank look forward to serving Springfield residents now and in the years to come. ❡

Giving back to the community has always been part of the Washington Mutual and Western Bank history. Pictured here are two participants in the company's School Savings Program, which has been teaching children the value of saving and money management since 1923. The School Savings program continues to thrive today, with hundreds of children participating in the Springfield area.

UNIVERSITY OF OREGON

Although it was the members of the Oregon Legislative Assembly who passed a bill in 1872 establishing a state university in Eugene, it was a grassroots effort by the community that kept alive the dream that would one day create the University of Oregon.

Money was scarce in the early years, so the local community of Eugene ambitiously agreed to supply the building if the legislature agreed in-kind to locate the university within its reach. "The Building" was planned to be larger and grander than any other building in town, so this determined community organized a door-to-door campaign to its 1,000 residents, producing contributions ranging from livestock to labor.

When the doors of Deady Hall opened officially for classes on October 16, 1876, with John Wesley Johnson serving as president, the university was in debt. That first year, five faculty members offered a handful of classes to 177 students. For the following two decades, students could earn degrees in either "the classical" or "the scientific" area. Each degree demanded six years of intense study and required such courses as Latin, Greek, and astronomy.

In 1893, Charles Hiram Chapman became the university's second president and liberalized the curriculum by introducing elective courses. That same year, the fourth building on campus, Friendly Hall, was built to serve as a coed dormitory. Men were required to enter the building from the south and the women from the north.

A year later in March 1894, the University of Oregon football team played its first game, beating Albany College, now Lewis and Clark College, 40-0.

By the turn of the century, the university's student population had grown to 456 students, and it was during these years that students formed the Associated Students of the University of Oregon (ASUO) and published the first issue of "Oregon Weekly," which in 1920 became the "Oregon Daily Emerald."

A spirit of community activism—both locally and nationally—began to emerge in the early 1900s, and it has proven to be an important part of the university's history. During World War I, a British officer named Col. John Leader helped transform the University of Oregon into a military training ground to teach men how to march in formation and properly handle a rifle.

During World War II, it was not unusual to see students marching to class. Staff and students were dedicated to the war effort, sponsoring scrap drives, fundraisers, and blood drives through the American Red Cross. In 1944, the University of Oregon gained notoriety by raising more money for war bonds than any other college or university in the nation.

This activism continued throughout the 1960s, when sit-ins staged in Johnson Hall became the popular venue for students wishing to express themselves. And in 1994, the University of Oregon's record-breaking effort to register voters gained national attention and earned the campus the distinction of being one of the nation's ten "most activist campuses."

Through the decades, the university has diversified to serve the needs of not only its students but the public as well. Today, more than 125 years after its inception, the campus population has grown to approximately 17,000 students and 2,400 teaching and research faculty members and graduate student assistants. The UO Alumni Association—organized in 1879 to "promote continued involvement after graduation" among the university's first five graduates—now serves more than 150,000 alumni and friends in 15 countries. ❺

All classrooms and facilities at the University of Oregon offer state-of-the-art technology for enhancing teaching and learning. In the Knight Library, (pictured) electronic resources provide students, faculty, and community members with access to a diverse range of materials, including contemporary and historical references to the sciences, humanities, and social sciences.

High-back wooden desks were characteristic of classrooms during the early years of the University of Oregon.

MCDONALD CANDY CO.

The Eugene-Springfield area has changed dramatically since Weir McDonald established his candy and tobacco company in Eugene in 1928. McDonald began the company four years earlier in Medford.

Although few residents may have met the 100-year-old McDonald in person, many may have seen his film work on television over the years.

McDonald was a world-renowned big game hunter and collected more than 125 world-class trophies. When he was not hunting with a gun, he used a camera. His work has been featured in the film Luxury Safaris and the movie King Solomon's Mines.

Several years ago, McDonald donated his trophies to the Tucson Wildlife Museum in Tucson, Arizona.

McDonald is the son of a Medford banker. He delivered groceries from his bicycle as a young boy. When he was 25, his father helped him get started in Medford as a tobacco dealer.

His company was located next door to a candy dealer, and eventually the two businesses merged.

McDonald Candy Co. opened on Olive Street in Eugene in 1928. It has served Springfield ever since.

The company outgrew its original facility in the 1930s and moved to the corner of Fourth and Willamette Streets near the train depot.

In 1959, the company moved to its present location at 2350 West Broadway.

Over the years, McDonald expanded the company to include restaurant supplies, food, beer, and wine, along with candy and tobacco. The beer and wine division was named Western Beverage Co., which today is the area's exclusive distributor of Anheuser-Busch products.

The company supplies its products to hundreds of Springfield area grocery stores, taverns, restaurants, and other establishments.

Weir McDonald still works every day at the company he built from the ground up. Today, it is one of the most successful wholesaling operations in Oregon.

The company currently employs more than 300 workers and markets its wide variety of products from Salem to Newport and to Eugene, Coos Bay, and south to the California border.

Company president, Rod Huey, carries on McDonald's proud tradition. Huey joined the company in 1966 while attending the University of Oregon. 🌰

Women and children spent long hours picking hops along with the men, but most considered it an excellent temporary job. Photo courtesy of the Springfield Museum.

Boats were bobbing in the lively flow of the McKenzie River during a Whitewater Parade. Photo courtesy of the Oregon State Highway Department.

Chapter Nine 9

1926-1950

A formal meeting of the Springfield chapter of the Altrusa Club in the 1950s, a national organization dedicated to charity. Photo courtesy of the Springfield Museum.

SPRINGFIELD AREA
CHAMBER OF COMMERCE

with the National Recovery Act during the Great Depression, bank services for the city, support for a sales tax in Oregon, citywide beautification, and many other projects.

This very comprehensive approach to what should concern the business community has continued to this day with the modern Chamber remaining a very community-oriented organization.

Incorporation

The Springfield Chamber of Commerce became an official Oregon corporation March 29, 1949. It has continued to be a membership-based, non-profit education corporation. Springfield was still a small town in 1949, with only 9,488 citizens, one high school, one junior high school and three elementary schools, but the Chamber was far from a "small" organization.

Its incorporation re-energized the Chamber, whose membership had swelled to more than 300 local businesses, including the newly launched Weyerhaeuser Company investment in Springfield. The city was experiencing a significant growth period during the post World War II years and the Chamber's agenda reflected a town in transition—a city about to be born.

The Bob Smith Era

In the midst of this development and growth, the Chamber hired a young man to lead it as Executive Vice-President. That man was Bob Smith. It's unlikely that anyone in 1957 would guess that this young man would serve the Chamber for 33 uninterrupted years, a chamber record in Oregon!

During those years, the Chamber and the City of Springfield both grew dramatically. Bob Smith cared deeply about the people and businesses and championed Springfield as an emerging industrial leader within the state.

The story of the Springfield Chamber of Commerce mirrors the best of Springfield's business culture and community for the past 50 years. It is a fascinating story of people, progress, and pride told against the backdrop of a town that has evolved into a city.

The Chamber has honored personal leadership and promoted progress of its individual business members and the City of Springfield. The Chamber also takes pride in its leadership role in the Springfield and Eugene metro area.

The Chamber has been a good partner in building the Springfield community—a town that became a city without losing its direction and sense of quality of life for people and business.

The Early Years

The Chamber story really begins much earlier than its official incorporation date in March 1949. As early as January 1933, the Chamber began its recorded history as a loosely-knit businessmen's club formed to "get things done." The early emphasis on "getting things done" carries through to the vision statement of the modern-day Chamber: "Building Our Community Together."

During the early years, the Chamber tackled such varied issues as: the route of the Pacific Highway through Springfield, economic development, cooperation

The Chamber responded to the growth of Springfield by promoting early development of the Gateway area and the hotel industry, as well as supporting the formation of the Willamalane Park and Recreation District, and the creation of McKenzie-Willamette Hospital.

The Bob Smith years saw the industrial base of Springfield grow to become the second largest industrial center in the state after Portland. The lumber industry, especially, led the way to strong economic and community growth during much of the 1960s and 1970s.

In addition to fostering economic growth, during this period, the Chamber continued to maintain its close community ties. The Springfield Christmas Parade, "The Oldest and Coldest in Oregon," is an unbroken tradition that dates back to 1953. The parade, in addition to good, positive relationships with city government, Willamalane Park and Recreation District, the Springfield Public School District and other community institutions, has kept the Chamber close to the people of Springfield. Chamber leadership, represented by a strong board of directors and committee chairs, fought for a good business climate and a high quality of life in the fast growing city of Springfield. Board presidents of this period led a Chamber that had great energy and growth, but also a Chamber that continued to put people and leadership first.

When Bob Smith came to the Chamber in 1957, there were 14,000 residents in Springfield. By the time he retired in 1990, more than 44,000 people called Springfield home and several thousand others lived just outside the city limits, but worked at Springfield businesses. Bob Smith's personal leadership and impact was such during this era that at the time of his retirement, he was widely known in the Springfield and Eugene area respectfully as "Mr. Springfield."

The 1990s

In 1993, the Springfield Chamber moved into the historic Springfield Depot Building at 101 South A Street. The move—crafted by Chamber leadership, the Depot Foundation, and the new Executive Vice-President Jean DeYoung—was significant, as the Springfield Depot became the official Springfield Visitors Center.

The Chamber began a long and fruitful relationship with the City of Springfield supplying visitor services and acting as an effective 'Welcome to Springfield' at its Depot location near the city's western gateway.

Much of the Chamber's focus in the early 1990s was on the strength and direction of the organization. The Chamber and its boards of directors effectively helped guide the chamber members and the community toward a very positive and successful rebound from what had

been a significant economic downturn in the state's— and Springfield's—economy.

Springfield Chamber of Commerce—
Building Our Community Together

In 1995, the City of Springfield and the local business community were once again on the move and growing. A completely new Chamber staff was brought on-board to not only convey and translate the excitement of the new growth to the membership, but to help define a new leadership role for the Chamber.

The local economy was diversifying rapidly with expansions in the high-tech industry, financial services, and the visitor industry, and the Chamber had a role to play in identifying new opportunities and acting as a catalyst for positive change in Springfield.

The Board of Directors and staff of the Chamber, led by Executive Vice-President Dan Egan, began working on programs that drew on the historic strengths of the organization—good community relationships, a strong volunteer base, and a pride in Springfield. It was a necessary new energy that spoke to the Chamber's growing membership base.

Today the Chamber leads the way with new initiatives, such as the Glenwood Project, the Springfield Renaissance Development Corporation, and the Jasper-Natron Development. The Chamber continues to seek partnerships based on an optimistic future for both the businesses and citizens of Springfield.

Indeed, the story of the Springfield Chamber of Commerce does mirror the best of the past and the best hopes of a bright future in Springfield—a city that is maturing and coming into its own as we approach a new millennium. The Chamber, with its nearly 600 members and leaders, applauds the progress of the past and continues to play a vital leadership role in shaping a successful and exciting future for the business community and the larger community of Springfield. ✿

REED'S FUEL AND TRUCKING

Through world wars, arson fires, hard times, and four generations, the trucks always kept rolling at Reed's Fuel and Trucking.

Last year, the company's fleet of almost 60 trucks covered more than 4.46 million miles of highway in Oregon, Washington, and Idaho, using 948,000 gallons of diesel along the way.

The family-owned company has come even further from its humble beginnings since William Reed and his son, Alvin, founded the business 59 years ago.

William and Alvin both were broke when they brought their wives to Springfield in 1940. A prolonged strike at the mill where they were employed in Toledo, Oregon, left them virtually penniless.

A friend of William's convinced them a hardworking man could make a living in Springfield, with its abundance of mills.

William and his wife, Floy, and Alvin with his young bride, Dorothy, both traded in their cars on two trucks.

One was a 1940 Chevrolet truck that cost $825. A 1939 GMC cost $695. "We must have financed them because I know we didn't have any money," Dorothy Reed said.

The business originally began as Reed's Transfer. William and Alvin initially planned to go into the moving business, but after about a year realized there wasn't much of a market for that in Springfield.

Instead, they began hauling wood and sawdust to residents.

"In those days, they burned wood to cook and heat," Dorothy said. William and Alvin put in long days keeping the business afloat.

"If a truck broke down, they would work on it all night to get it going," Dorothy remembers.

Reed's Transfer landed a vital contract in the early 1940s hauling 4-foot slab wood to Springfield High School. It was used to heat the building. A cord of basic firewood cost $3.50 at the time. Sawdust retailed for about 90 cents per unit.

Alvin was drafted into the U.S. Army in 1944 and served 18 months during World War II. In his absence, Dorothy got grandmother to baby-sit, hopped in her husband's truck, and delivered wood to customers. At age 77, Dorothy is still active in the company business and goes to work every day.

The company name changed to Reed's Fuel Co. in 1948, and the business began to grow.

Weyerhaeuser Co. opened a Springfield sawmill in 1949. Reed's began hauling logs to the mill as soon as it opened. George Weyerhaeuser managed the mill. He and Alvin soon became good friends.

"If it hadn't been for Weyerhaeuser, we wouldn't be here," Dorothy said. The company proudly displays a cut of timber from the last log Weyerhaeuser's sawmill processed before closing in 1991.

By the early 1950s, the company was operating a half-dozen trucks, including one fuel oil truck. Many Springfield residents had switched to burning fuel oil for heat, instead of sawdust or wood.

One of Reed's distinguished customers was the Springfield Hotel, a massive facility for its day located at Second and Main Streets downtown.

"The lady who ran that hotel was so cross I was scared of her," Dorothy said. But Alvin and William got along well with the cantankerous proprietor and convinced her to rent them space at the rear of the building.

A desk, chair, telephone, and window providing a view of the nearby railroad tracks made up Reed Fuel Co.'s first office.

Dorothy remembers waving at the train engineers during the next two years as they passed by hauling logs to the Booth Kelly sawmill. "Business wasn't that good."

In the mid-1950s, the company moved to more spacious accommodations at 242 Main Street in the same building currently standing at the address.

Reed's sold the fuel oil portion of its business to Marshall's, which shared office space with them downtown. Marshall's still operates in Springfield from an office on Olympic Street.

A few years later, Reed's moved to new accommodations at 122 N. Fifth Street and began hauling lumber from area mills.

One large job involved hauling the lumber used to build the new Springfield High School.

By now, Alvin was running the company on his own. Its fleet had grown to approximately 10 trucks.

Reed's built a truck shop on some isolated acreage at 14th Street and Mohawk Boulevard.

The State of Oregon took the property in the early 1960s to make way for Interstate 105, using the eminent domain law.

Oregon Department of Transportation officials actually dedicated the highway in 1973.

Reed's purchased a seven-acre parcel at 4080 Commercial Ave. in 1968 and built another truck shop on the site shortly after.

Four years later, the company completed its office building and has operated from the site ever since.

Other milestones passed in the 1960s. Reed's bought its first diesel truck in 1963 for $10,968. In 1997, the company paid $75,753 for a diesel truck.

Later that decade, Reed's hauled the first load of wood chips ever to arrive at Boise Cascade Co.'s new Salem plant. They came from Cone Lumber Co. in Goshen.

The early 1970s brought rapid growth and prosperity to Reed's. By 1975, the company's fleet more than doubled from 20 in the late 1960s to 47. The fleet would increase to almost 60 by decade's end and has remained constant ever since.

Reed's never missed a beat during the gasoline shortages that hit the nation in the mid-1970s. By then, Alvin's son, Gary, had worked his way through the ranks and would soon be named president, actually taking over the helm in 1980. He started as a truck driver about 1968.

Business was booming when the fuel crisis hit. Gary remembers how the fuel rationing presented both challenges and opportunities.

Reed's had a contract with ARCO to buy fuel directly off the pipeline. "They put us on quotas so we could only end up with so much even though we had been with them for ten years," Gary Reed said. It wasn't going to be enough.

The company was running 60 trucks and needed approximately 5,000 gallons of fuel a day to haul wood chips, sawdust, lumber, and the latest hot product—Presto logs—to customers in Oregon, Washington, and Idaho.

Junction City-based businessman Jerry Brown was able to supplement Reed's fuel supply through the crisis. Brown was known in the industry as a "jobber," or broker between many suppliers and customers.

A new agreement with Brown ensured the trucks would have enough fuel. But another serious problem arose.

Employees, or coworkers as Reed always refers to them, were having trouble obtaining enough gasoline for their personal vehicles to get to work each day. Some coworkers lived as far away as Cottage Grove and Albany.

"Needless to say, that was a real concern. Without drivers, we couldn't serve our customers," Gary Reed said. The company supplied coworkers with access to the card-lock systems for their vehicle use to and from work when necessary.

Eventually, the fuel crisis passed, and Reed's kept its fleet busy.

"The Presto log business was wonderful. Weyerhaeuser was making them," Dorothy said. "We kept one truck busy all day five or six days a week during the winter just hauling Presto logs. We hauled them to Albany, Salem, and locally."

Reed's diversified again in the early 1980s. The company needed to find new market niches as a major recession clamped down on the timber industry that had supported Reed's and much of Springfield for decades.

They began hauling steel, machinery, and general commodities on flatbed trucks.

"We wouldn't have diversified if so many of the mills hadn't closed down," Dorothy said. "It was good for us to be able to do that."

The company took on its current name, Reed's Fuel & Trucking, in the mid-1980s to more closely identify with the new image.

"A lot of people thought, and still do today, that we're a fuel business," company vice president Jason Reed said.

Meanwhile, Springfield officially recognized Alvin Reed for his years of community service. The Springfield Area Chamber of Commerce named Alvin Reed "Springfield's First Citizen" in 1982. Reed served on the Springfield City Council for nine years, primarily in the 1950s.

When Reed left the council in December 1958, Springfield Mayor Edward C. Harms Jr. wrote him a letter of appreciation for his service to the community.

"It is my personal opinion that you were the best councilman we have had during my association with the city," the Mayor Harms wrote.

Reed later served five years on the Rainbow Water District Board of Directors. He served a term as president of the Lane County Chamber of Commerce and was a longtime member of the Lions Club, Elks Club, and Masonic Lodge.

When he passed away in 1991, numerous friends came together to develop a memorial in his honor.

Reed's Fuel & Trucking and a host of other participants refurbished an old rail car into mint condition and donated it to the Springfield Chamber of Commerce.

The rail car now is located at the Springfield Depot just off South A Street.

Springfield Chamber of Commerce executive vice president Dan Egan said the rail car, which was donated in 1993, represents part of the city's heritage.

Dorothy said it is a fitting memorial to her husband.

Jason Reed represents a fourth generation to carry on the family business his grandfather started.

Reed began working for the company in the early 1980s during his high school years. He joined the ranks full time in 1988 after graduating from college. He drove trucks, worked as a dispatcher, and did just about anything else that was necessary.

"He started at the bottom and got a lot of encouragement from his grandfather," Dorothy said of her grandson.

Dan Leavitt joined the company in 1987 and is one of four stockholders, along with Jason, Gary, and Dorothy Reed.

Leavitt comes from a trucking family himself.

His grandfather started a Springfield-based trucking company in 1946.

Leavitt entered the trucking industry full-time after graduating from college.

Gary Reed recruited him to design computer software programs for truck maintenance and other aspects of the industry.

"There wasn't a lot of software out there for the trucking industry. We kind of designed our own package to meet our needs," Leavitt said.

Creative software programming also helped computerize the bookkeeping part of the business.

Those kinds of innovations help management organize a company that operates in perpetual motion.

Reed's Fuel & Trucking runs 24 hours a day, seven days a week. It's been that way as long as Jason can remember.

Dorothy says she can't remember a time when Reed's allowed its service to be interrupted.

Not even a devastating arson fire on October 8, 1995, interrupted service. The Sunday early morning fire gutted the office and caused $400,000 damage.

"We were open for business at 6 a.m. the following day," Jason Reed said. They ran dispatch and other services out of a cramped garage until they could bring modular buildings in.

Looking back to the company's beginning, Dorothy says the Reeds were fortunate to have found Springfield many years ago.

Alvin Reed moved to Oregon originally from Cairo, Nebraska, where he was born and raised on a 206-acre farm.

Reed arrived in Oregon knowing what it was like to be poor. The family lost the farm and just about everything else in The Great Depression.

Upon their arrival in Toledo, William and his family moved in with William's brother until he could get back on his feet financially.

It all worked out in the end, Dorothy said.

"Springfield has been very good to us. I feel very fortunate that we came to Springfield, made our homes, raised our family, and built our business here." ●

ROSBORO LUMBER COMPANY

T.W. (Whit) Rosborough, a successful Southern pine sawmill operator, began the Caddo River Lumber Company in Arkansas in the 1900s and was general manager until 1939. Some time before 1930, Rosborough acquired a large parcel of timberland near Mapleton, Oregon, where he planned to build a sawmill. Prior to beginning construction of the mill, however, he traded the parcel of timberland for larger holdings on the McKenzie River on Quartz Creek, near Finn Rock.

Along with 50 years of experience, Rosborough brought many employees from the Caddo River Lumber Company with him to Oregon to start up his new mill. The men, tried and true employees of Rosborough's mills in the towns of Rosboro, Forester, and Glenwood, Arkansas, moved out West—bringing their families with them.

Whit Rosborough retired in 1945, selling his interests to Mr. and Mrs. Beuford S. Cole, Mr. and Mrs. R. T. Watts, Mr. Spencer R. Collins, and Mr. Vernon Williams. Prior to the sale, Cole was general manager, Tom Watts served as mill superintendent, and Vernon Williams was woods superintendent. Spencer Collins operated an accounting firm in Eugene. Paul B. Cole, son of Beuford Cole, became general manager following the death of his father in 1958.

Rosboro's first business offices were in the Arcade Building at Fifth and Main Streets in downtown Springfield. The office was relocated in the early 1950s to its present location in the old Maple School building, directly north of the mill on Main Street.

Sawmill and Plants

Construction of the sawmill, which is located on the former Springfield Airport site, began in 1939 and was completed and in operation by June 1940. An article in an April 1940 issue of The Springfield News observed: "One of the West's most modern sawmills, under construction for the past year at Springfield by the Rosboro Lumber Company, is now in operation. While it is not one of the largest mills as computed by the board foot cut on the head rig daily, the new machines and up-to-date design make this new, streamlined plant outstanding in the lumber industry." This mill would soon become known as one of Springfield's largest and most well-established businesses—Rosboro Lumber Company.

The original sawmill, including plant, wigwam burner, and pond, covered nearly 40 acres and was designed to cut 150,000 board feet, per day. Employing about 100 workers, Rosboro was self-sufficient with energy created from its own three-stack power plant and two steam turbines. Today, the mill still produces steam for operating veneer dryers, steam vats, and the dry kilns, but now purchases electricity from Springfield Utility Board. The company began an aggressive program of modernization and expansion to upgrade its plants for greater efficiency and to increase volumes into other products, which continues today. From its original single-lumber operation, Rosboro has grown into one of the few integrated forest products operations in Oregon. The company has evolved from being a small sawmill in the 1940s, producing 40 million board feet per year, to an integrated plant covering 60 acres that has two sawmills, as well as veneer, plywood, and glulam beam plants.

The company continues to modernize, responding to the ongoing changes in the timber supply, as well as the demands of the marketplace. Computer programs and electronic imaging systems (scanners) control much of today's equipment, a dramatic change from the early years when employees did all the production functions manually.

Beginning in the 1970s, Rosboro began a program that enabled modification of the sawmills and veneer plant to handle the smaller log sizes and timber types. For example, in 1975, Rosboro built one of the first small-log sawmills in Lane County. Rosboro's transition to small logs had thus begun long before the supply of old-growth logs diminished.

Forestry, Logging, Timber Supply

Rosboro obtains its log supply from fee-owned lands, various purchased timber sales of the U.S. Forest Service, Bureau of Land Management, states, counties, and private timberland owners. Contract logging is utilized for much of the timber harvesting. Rosboro has mobile logging equipment and a truck fleet, which are used in internal and outside contract logging programs. Although Rosboro had 20,000 acres of timberland when it first began, by 1960 this had grown to 23,000 acres. Since then, Rosboro has continued to add timberland acreage and now has a substantial tree farm with units located in 11 counties.

Rosboro has an outstanding timberland management record. The company's chief forester for many years, Dave Burwell, established high goals in forestry and utilization, which have continued and even been further improved. Forestry and growing trees remain high priorities for Rosboro. Beginning with superior seeds grown in a cooperative nursery, planting, thinning, precommercial thinning, fertilizing programs, and harvest, strictly state-of-the-art methods are used to maximize timber growth.

Products and Philosophy

Employees are always considered the company's "number one resource," and Rosboro has many second, and even third generation, employees. Long-term employees are one of the greatest assets of any company. Rosboro has always provided a safe place for its employees and places great emphasis on safety programs and

employee health. Management involvement and team efforts by employees continue to keep the company's accident rates and injury levels far below the industry average. The Rosboro manufacturing complex now covers 60 acres within Springfield city limits and employs close to 400 people.

Rosboro provides a wide variety of products, including dimensional lumber and studs for the home building market; veneer, for plywood and LVL (laminated veneer lumber) production; as well as laminated beams for heavy construction. The company serves customers throughout the United States, as well as in Canada, Australia, and Japan.

Timber continues to be the basic raw material for all of Rosboro's products, and timber supplies have changed drastically. Due to the listing of the spotted owl, and other pressures, the U.S. Forest Service and Bureau of Land Management have greatly reduced the amount of timber available for sale from public lands. This scarcity has caused log prices to greatly increase due to the intense competition for logs. Since the spotted owl listing, many mills have closed and gone out of business. Rosboro's aggressive timberland acquisition and management programs have allowed the company to continue through this difficult transition period.

Product diversity and responding to changing conditions continue to be the primary goals of the company—as they have been since Rosboro's inception. As President Paul Cole stated, "We're in this business to serve our customers over the long term. That philosophy is reflected in everything we produce and every management decision we make."

Current Executive Management

The current executive management team includes Paul B. Cole, president; David Weza, vice president; Gordon Culbertson, vice president of timberlands; and Donald Hawkins, controller. ✪

SPRINGFIELD QUARRY
ROCK PRODUCTS

Mr. Wilson Jewett and Mr. Bill Reeves started the company in the 1920s as the Springfield Sand and Gravel Company. This company took river rock from the Middle Fork of the Willamette River at a location approximately two-thirds of a mile to the east of the present-day rock quarry. The sand and gravel company provided a much-needed product for the growing timber harvesting and product manufacturing industry, as well as the related housing and service industry requirements.

A wage book from the mid-1920s shows the company employed up to nine people, with wages running from $1.20 to $4.20 per day, depending on whether the employee was a laborer or machine operator.

In the 1960s and early 1970s, the quarry went through a significant expansion and increase in the number of products. In the mid-1960s, the quarry was purchased by brothers Larry and Harry Weiss. In addition to railroad ballast, the company started to produce two other products, one being drainage rock for home and farm improvements such as driveways and drainage fields. Another product, called "the logger special," was rock specifically produced to use on forestry roads. With large-scale production of "the logger special," the quarry played an important part in the expansion of the area timber harvesting industry.

Maintenance shops were added to the site in the 1960s to provide the company with a greater capacity to service its own growing quarry equipment and truck inventory. A fire destroyed the office in the 1960s as well, and the current office was built as a replacement. Equipment used prior to the late 1970s was cable shovels and belly dump trucks.

From the late 1970s until the early 1980s, wheel loaders replaced the shovels in the pit. In addition to jaw and cone crushers, impact crushers were brought on-site to increase production. Providing stone to lumber companies for backfilling old timber millponds became important accounts to the company.

The company became a hard rock producer in the late 1940s when it began quarrying operations at the present location on south 18th Street as Springfield Quarry Rock Products. Rock produced from the quarry is igneous basalt rock, which is rock solidified from a volcanic molten state. At that time, the quarry produced and sold railroad ballast to the Southern Pacific Railroad, which was expanding its service area to keep pace with the booming timber manufacturing industry. The City of Springfield tripled its size between 1940-50. Rock products played a necessary part in the construction boom.

In the mid-1980s, the truck weighing system was changed from a large dial weight read-out to a computerized weighing system.

By the late 1980s, the quarry provided seven products for home and commercial site improvement and development, road construction, timber, and railroad industries.

Mobile equipment used today includes rubber-tired wheel loaders for moving material, bulldozers for excavation and material movement. The company has its own truck and trailer fleet.

Mining the rock involves ripping rock where possible from the quarry face using bulldozers. Planned and carefully executed blasting is also required in places to remove the rock from the hillside. Once the rock is removed from the hill, it is transported down to the rock processing facility.

The rock processing equipment includes a primary jaw crusher, a secondary cone crusher, and finishing impact crushers with numerous screens and blending chutes. An operator using closed-circuit television monitors the rock processing operations. The operator can make changes from his enclosed viewing station. Once processed, the rock is placed in a stockpile of a particular product size and specification.

Today, the quarry has 33 employees and produces more than 15 products, ranging from landscaping boulders to machine-select riprap, railroad ballast, drainage rock of various sizes, base rock, fill material, and road construction material meeting specific rigorous standards required by the Oregon Department of Transportation, the U.S. Forest Service, the Bureau of Land Management, and county and city regulatory requirements.

The quarry service area has expanded from just within the city of Springfield to serve an area with an approximate 50-mile radius of the quarry. The location and ability to make a quality product make the quarry a valuable resource to the future industrial, civic, commercial, and residential expansion of the Eugene and Springfield metropolitan area. ◗

WILDISH COMPANIES

T.C. and Verna with the crushing plant at the Wildish Sand & Gravel Co. facility in Glenwood.

The Depression was hard on families.

It was hard on the Thomas C. Wildish family. In 1934, at the age of 46, Thomas, his wife, Verna, and their five sons and six daughters left the drought-stricken plains of North Dakota and headed to the lushness of the Willamette Valley with hopes of beginning a new life.

They probably could never have imagined that six decades later the name Wildish would be associated with a multifaceted, multimillion-dollar company that would be credited with the construction of almost every major road and a variety of other projects in Lane County.

On the Wildish family's arrival in Oregon, "T.C.," as he was called, traded in his pickup for a 1935 Ford truck nicknamed "Old Fiver" and began hauling loads of gravel for whoever would hire him. A son, Norm Wildish, was his first "employee," and together they hauled sand and gravel for Lane County at $1.25 an hour, which was good money in those days.

By the next year, Wildish had purchased two trucks, followed by three more the following year.

Norm Wildish said his father was fond of buying Fords.

"I think it's because Dad built business relationships with certain people, but he also had an affinity for Henry Ford," Norm Wildish said. "He liked the way Henry Ford did business."

The Wildish Company continued its growth, and by 1941, the delivery business had expanded to nearly a dozen trucks, with drivers hauling loads around the state.

By the mid-1940s, Wildish branched out, buying a bulldozer and excavating equipment. The firm could now do underground utility work, and for many years was able to work autonomously on a project, doing its own excavation, rocking, paving, and trucking.

T.C. purchased the company's Glenwood site on Franklin Boulevard in 1945, and in addition to sand and gravel land along the Coast and Middle forks of the Willamette River, he now owned more than 1,000 acres in the Mount Pisgah area.

In 1947, the company bought its own gravel crushing plant, followed by the purchase of a small asphalt plant in 1951.

Now able to be a "one-stop road construction operation," Wildish contracted with the City of Springfield to pave between Main and E Streets and 21st and 28th. A later project, on Mill Street between Main and G Streets, was the first of its kind using water-treated crushed rock, a process which set the standard for street construction at the time.

In 1960, Wildish acquired Cascade Concrete Company and adopted the company's Three Sisters logo as its own. The company continued to thrive and completed many notable projects, such as the Knickerbocker Bike Bridge, resurfacing at the Eugene Airport, and log yard improvements for timber mills such as Oregon Cedar, Weyerhaeuser Co., Clear Fir, and Booth-Kelly.

Through the 1970s-80s, along with major street work, Wildish Construction Co. was the general contractor for the Glenwood solid waste transfer station and the Stadium Club at Autzen Stadium. Projects were also completed at the University of Oregon, including Streisinger Hall, Willamette Hall, and the Chiles Center. Wildish has also done projects for Portland State University, Oregon State University, and Western Oregon University.

In the early 1980s, Wildish Companies moved its main plant from Glenwood to its current location on County Farm Road, off Coburg Road.

Of T.C. Wildish's sons, James Wildish is company president; Thomas E. Wildish is chairman of the board of directors; Norman Wildish is vice-chairman; and Jim's sons Mike and Steve share vice presidency status with nephew Bill Wildish.

Although Thomas C. Wildish died in 1963, three generations of Wildish family members have shared the company's vision to produce high-quality products in a profitable and safe manner, while maximizing long-term returns on assets. As a leader in its industry, the company continues to fulfill obligations to customers, shareholders, subcontractors, and suppliers, while at the same time recognizing the contributions of its employees and their families. Wildish also has a commitment to respect the natural environment.

The Eugene Water and Electric Board contracted with Wildish to build a 400-foot flume at its Leaburg dam to aid fish passage. The flume channels salmon and other species from the power canal into the McKenzie River, increasing their chances of survival and successful migration to the ocean.

Wildish evolved from hauling gravel and digging basements in the 1940s, to road construction in the 1950s, to putting in subdivisions, hydro-facilities, and wastewater treatment plants in the 1970s-80s, to multifaceted projects into the 1990s.

To its honor, Wildish has been the recipient of the "Governor's Award for Corporate Excellence" and the "Environmental Award" from the Asphalt Pavement Association of Oregon, as well as numerous awards from the Oregon Concrete and Aggregate Producers Association and community public works departments.

The company undertakes over 250 projects each season and has done work across Oregon, and in Washington, California, Arizona, Idaho, and Nevada.

President James Wildish notes that the company is "resource oriented and always looking for opportunities in the Northwest for growth."

"Whether constructing bridges, buildings, or streets, what's unique about Wildish is that we provide one-source construction service. We can supply the rock, put in a road and utilities, and build the facility. Not many companies can offer all that."

Whether it's the weekend do-it-yourselfer who needs a load of gravel for a home improvement project, or a corporation negotiating a multimillion-dollar project, Wildish continues to serve its customers in the manner of T.C. Wildish—with integrity, honesty, and dedication to "do the job right." ◗

Mike Wildish, Jim Wildish, Bill Wildish, Tom Wildish, Steve Wildish, Norm Wildish at the Eugene Airport which was renovated by the Wildish Companies.

WILLAMALANE PARK
& RECREATION DISTRICT

Families enjoy the Lively Park Swim Center wave pool and water slide.

(right) c.1950s line of families waiting to use the Willamalane pool.

With a growing population of nearly 4,000 residents, by the mid-1940s it was time for Springfield to start thinking about developing parks.

In September 1944, Lane County District Attorney William S. Fort (later to become Judge Fort) asked the people of Springfield and Glenwood to vote on a measure proposing a special purpose park and recreation district.

With the bank of the Willamette River flowing nearby, and assuming someday the district would encompass all of Lane County, Fort selected the name "Willamalane."

In the same election, voters chose Dr. Melville S. Jones, E.H. "Gene" Silke, and William Earl James to serve as the district's first board of directors. Silke was considered an added bonus to the board (said Fort in a 1982 interview), "...because he [Silke] was very well liked by the people of Springfield and he was an excellent school superintendent."

In Willamalane's first fiscal year, which began the following July, the district had neither budget nor property.

By 1945, Walter Hansen was hired as Willamalane's first superintendent with a proposed annual budget of $25,000, and Willamalane Park in Springfield was purchased for $200 and James Park, in Glenwood, for $10.

In 1947, the American Legion had raised $50,000 in bonds, donations, labor, and materials to begin construction on the new Veterans' Memorial Building, but by 1949, the Legion had run out of funds. The unfinished building, along with its $6,000 liability, was donated to Willamalane.

Soon after, voters approved a $285,000 bond issue for a pool and community center.

The Memorial Building was completed at an additional cost of $80,000 and was dedicated on May 30, 1951. Willamalane Park was developed with the aid of a $25,000 gift from the Booth Kelly Lumber Company.

Willamalane Pool officially opened July 4, 1951. In 1961, after nearly a decade of tolerating Oregon's wet weather, voters approved a $285,000 bond measure to cover the pool. (The roof came off again later due to structural problems, but voters approved a $4.7-million bond measure in November 1998 to reroof the pool in 1999.)

Park development continued through the 1970s, including the purchase of Dorris Ranch property, and a $1.3-million bond passed in 1976 to fund construction of the Willamalane Senior Adult Activity Center near Island Park.

Around the same time, Mr. and Mrs. Jack B. Lively donated $100,000 to Willamalane to be used for promotion of parks, recreation, and open spaces. Some years later, a foundation was established, and some of the funds were used for the kiddie pool and water umbrella at Lively Park Swim Center and a new playground at Willamalane Park.

In the early 1980s, school recreation programs were revised and expanded, and in 1982, Daniel Plaza (the current superintendent) was hired as Willamalane's seventh superintendent.

In 1989, the Lively Park Swim Center was built, complete with the Northwest's first indoor wave pool, a lap pool, a 26-person Jacuzzi™, a family swim area, a 136-foot water slide, and a kiddie pool.

From two parks in 1945 to 32 parks and five facilities in 1999, Willamalane Park and Recreation District continues to work under the philosophy of supplying leisure alternatives for people of all age groups, interests, and economic status. ❧

MARSHALL'S INC.

Marshall W. Dannen Sr. and Ann Dannen ventured into business in August 1948 when they bought an oil truck and the home-heating portion of his former employer's company. They started with 238 residential customers. By 1950, "Marshall's Oil" customer base had grown to 1,000 and had added two more oil trucks.

Dannen hired firemen to help deliver the heating oil to customers, as their shift work was compatible with delivery schedules.

Marshall Dannen II started working for his parents' company at age 15. Within a year, he was making fuel oil deliveries and servicing customers' oil furnaces. His mother, Ann, often rode with him on delivery runs. Ann also handled all the accounting and bookkeeping for the young, growing business.

Through the 1960s, Marshall's Oil remained dedicated to providing the best possible service to customers. During the Willamette Valley's famous "big snow" of 1969, freezing temperatures gripped the area for about two weeks. Marshall's picked up its employees in four-wheel drive vehicles and brought them through the snow to the office on 28th Street. The staff worked around the clock when necessary to ensure customers didn't run out of heating oil. Company wives brought in food while employees and management lived at the office for all intents and purposes until the icy weather gave way.

Marshall II helped put himself through college delivering heating oil and furnace repairs. In 1972 he borrowed money from his parents to begin an insulation-contracting firm.

The resulting "Marshall's Insulation" marked the first time Marshall's Inc. had diversified into new markets. Within two years, Marshall's Insulation was one of the area's largest insulation contractors in an industry that would soon become huge.

A national emphasis on oil conservation in the early '70s placed an emphasis on energy conservation and insulation. Marshall's Insulation business employed 20 full-time installers in 1978 and 1979, when the industry was at its peak.

Marshall Sr. retired in 1974. Ann followed three years later. When their son and his wife, Gail, bought out the business, Marshall's began to diversify further.

In 1977 Marshall's moved from its office on 28th Street to more spacious accommodations on E Street, allowing the company to grow. Marshall's moved to its current location on 42nd and Olympic streets in 1995. They built a new facility on the site to accommodate a progressive company.

Today, six affiliated businesses operate under the parent company of Marshall's Inc.

Marshall's Inc. sells and services heating and air conditioning systems (electric, gas, oil, heat pumps) and natural gas and electric fireplaces as well as hot water heaters for residential and commercial installation. Marshall's operates a sheet metal shop, installs insulation (thermal and acoustical) for residential and commercial applications, and delivers fuel products, including gasoline and lube oils.

Overall, the company employs 60 people who serve thousands of customers with various products and services.

Marshall's is a major supplier of heating and cooling systems in new and retrofit construction projects.

Chad Dannen marked the family's third generation in the family business in 1992 and his sister, Michelle, transferred careers to join the forces in 1998. Seth, the youngest sibling, does advertising and clerical work for the company.

Marshall's was honored in 1997 as one of the top ten dealers in the nation to install and service Bryant HVAC equipment. Marshall's celebrated its 50th year in business in 1997 with an open house for their contractors, builders, and customers. ❂

SQUARE DEAL LUMBER

Jack Kuykendall started Square Deal Lumber in 1947 with five acres of land and a 1941 Chevrolet truck. It was hard work, but relatively simple, his son Bud Kuydendall remembers.

Jack picked up a unit of lumber varying in dimensions from local sawmills, then drove around town selling it. One man, one faithful truck, and a vision. Kuykendall quickly expanded his lumber yard into a full-service building materials store. By the early 1950s, he had opened two additional retail outlets—BiRite Lumber and River Road Building Supply—both in Eugene.

Bud Kuykendall began working for his father in the early 1950s after school, on weekends, and during the summers. He made 25 cents an hour to start. After

graduating from Eugene High School, he attended the University of Oregon on a basketball scholarship. His sister, Rosalyn, chose not to join the family business.

Bud joined Square Deal Lumber full-time in the mid-1960s after graduating from the University of Oregon. He became president of the company located at 4992 Main Street in the late 1980s.

More than a half-dozen other full-service building material stores have come and gone in Springfield since Square Deal Lumber opened. Today, Square Deal Lumber stands alone as Springfield's only lumber yard and building materials store.

Loyal employees, solid business practices, and some unusual services for customers provided the keys to Square Deal's longevity, Bud Kuykendall says.

"Satisfaction is guaranteed every order, every time," says Tim Wenzl, the company's general manager since the late 1980s. "We do it every time. Sometimes it does cost us money. But we do it every time."

They sell to commercial contractors, home builders, remodelers, and the general public. Employee longevity is another Square Deal trademark. Kuykendall said at least seven workers have retired from the company after long careers.

Yard manager Ron Weise and salesman Bob Sorter each have worked for the company more than 35 years. Employees showed their true loyalty when times were bad in the late 1970s and early '80s. A deep recession had slowed the timber industry to a crawl.

Bud remembers how his employees responded: "Nine (out of 10) of them came to me and said, 'Bud, we need a pay cut.'"

Only a few years before that, Square Deal narrowly escaped a massive tragedy while constructing a 32,000-square-foot warehouse on the existing building.

A severe windstorm hit while workers were trying to install roof trusses. The entire structure collapsed.

Through good times and bad, an unusual but long standing tradition remains at Square Deal. Every Wednesday, a worker makes free delivery runs up the McKenzie River as far as McKenzie Bridge, as well as free delivery to the Springfield-Eugene Metro Area.

Even the smallest order, such as a bag of nails or a hammer, is delivered free, Wenzl says. "We've been doing that for 52 years."

Square Deal Lumber does the vast majority of its business in Lane County, Kuykendall says.

The company has played a major role in helping Springfield grow, supplying building materials for hundreds of local projects. Square Deal also has sent its share of lumber overseas, supplying building materials for churches in South Africa, Fiji, and Guatemala. ◗

BRANDT FINANCE COMPANY

Al Brandt's first prospective customers never waited long to find out if they qualified for a loan.

Brandt normally set his sack lunch aside and opened his check book to see if he could loan them any money.

Looking back on those days 50 years later, Brandt says the simplicity of it all probably helped him make better loan decisions.

Laws and procedures have changed dramatically since Al opened Brandt Finance Company at 229 Main Street in November 21, 1948.

But Brandt's trademark personal service has endured five decades in downtown Springfield

At age 90, Brandt still works full time at his namesake business, now known as Brandt Financial Services, Inc. He does the books by hand, bucking the computer age trend. His customers are known by name not a number.

Brandt's financial services career began in his home town of Milwaukee, Wisconsin in 1929 when he went to work for a nationwide finance company.

The company moved Brandt west in 1931 and he moved to Eugene two years later to manage an office.

He met his wife, a school teacher named Helen Overman, and moved to Tacoma with her in 1939.

Five years later, Brandt was drafted into the US Army. He went through basic training at the age of 35 after spending 16 years behind a finance desk.

"They called me 'pops' because I was so old," Brandt says.

Army officials assigned Brandt to an infantry division. "I finally told them I can't see without my glasses and I was liable to shoot just about anybody," Brandt says. He ended up with an assignment in London with the Supreme Headquarters Allied Expeditionary Force (SHAEF) as part of Gen. Dwight D. Eisenhower's staff.

Brandt was 40 when he arrived back in Springfield. His daughter, B.J. was 10 months old. "I decided it was time to go into business for myself."

The business has moved twice since 1948. Brandt Financial Services, Inc. moved into its current office on North A Street in 1980.

B.J. Brandt joined her father's business during high school in 1965. She has been Al's business manager since 1979 and president since 1984.

Brandt's reputation for fair, personal service keeps a loyal customer base coming back.

Laws provide some loan guidelines, but Brandt remains a small business with no set rules for qualifying applicants.

Brandt does almost no advertising, instead relying on word of mouth to bring in new customers.

B.J. says her rapport with clients allows her to sometimes take extraordinary measures on their behalf.

She's there for them on a Friday night when a sudden death in family requires a trip across the country. On occasion, B.J. even wires additional funds for customers in emergency situations.

Community leaders have noticed Brandt's dedication to Springfield.

The Chamber of Commerce named Brandt Springfield's Distinguished Citizen in 1993. Oregon Gov. Tom McCall appointed Brandt to the first Lane Transit District Board of Directors in 1970.

The financial world has changed dramatically since Brandt started packing a lunch to that small office with no bathroom in 1948.

Brandt's ideas for service never did. ❂

SPRINGFIELD UTILITY BOARD

pringfield Utility Board (SUB) is a publicly owned utility that provides Springfield with water and electricity services. Keeping rates low, service reliable, and encouraging citizen participation has made SUB an integral part of the community. In fact, SUB customers receive an owner's manual that says: "It's your utility." SUB's operating philosophy has always been customer focused and "people-powered." Although people may assume it's always been that way, older residents may remember a time when that wasn't the case at all.

Electricity first came to Springfield in the early 1900s. Across the country, both privately owned and municipally owned utilities were forming. Early municipal systems often developed to provide street lighting, but Mountain States Power, the private company that sold Springfield residents electricity, refused to do anything about street lighting. Besides that, its rates were high and its service was hit-and-miss at best. Across the river, Eugene had solved similar problems by creating a customer-owned system in 1911. By the 1930s, Springfield residents who'd had enough of Mountain States' failure to meet community needs campaigned to create a utility of their own. The campaign spanned six elections and two recall attempts.

Finally, on June 24, 1949, an amendment to the City Charter authorized the creation of a customer-owned utility in Springfield. The next year, the City Charter transferred responsibility for the utility to an independent board of five citizens, the "City of Springfield Utility Board." Even today, SUB is one of only a handful of utilities operated by a citizen board.

Soon, the new utility had constructed a distribution system, and the two electrical systems—public and private—stood side-by-side in the streets of Springfield. For the next 25 years, SUB battled with Mountain States Power and its successor, Pacific Power & Light (PP&L), to provide a single, low-cost source of power.

Springfield residents Jack and Iona Hartman became the first customers of the new utility on September 5, 1950. The number of SUB customers grew steadily and sometimes dramatically, as in 1960, when SUB purchased the McKenzie Highway Water District and in 1965, when SUB bought out Eugene Water & Electric Board's electrical facilities in east Springfield.

SUB's reputation for reliability and service grew as well. After the Columbus Day Storm of 1962, one of the worst storms in local history, SUB crews restored power to every customer in only 24 hours.

In 1975, voters approved a $14-million bond allowing SUB to buy PP&L's electric and water facilities. The bond was repaid in 1995, giving the utility's customer-owners 100 percent equity in their power company.

Over the years, SUB has added other benefits to its services with conservation, weatherization, and payment programs. SUB also helped bring energy and water curriculum to Springfield schools. A recently completed 30-mile backbone for a fiber-optic system will help meet Springfield's future power needs. Yesterday, today, and tomorrow, working hard to keep rates low and reliability high, SUB plays an important part in the quality of life of its customer-owners and in the history of Springfield. ◗

Mid-'50s Springfield Utility Board of Directors: (left to right) Don Peglow, D.R. Offley, Ed Starr, Charles Buckel, and George Glidden.

1998—linemen lay the final section of a 30-mile fiber optic backbone currently used for high-speed data transmission and establishing the basis for meeting community needs in the future.

KNECHT'S AUTO PARTS

The story behind one of Oregon's most successful auto parts chains all started just after World War II with a travelling tire salesman who wanted to come home every night to his wife and four children. Nate Knecht was on the road constantly while working for Kelly Rubber Company in April 1947.

Kelly managers asked Knecht to find a new owner/manager for the company's Springfield store. A deal with the former investors fell through, forcing the store to close after only a few months.

Knecht found one quickly—himself. He renamed the ailing young business Knecht's Tire & Oil Co. It was located near 33rd and Main Streets, about a block from his home.

Originally, the business served as a truck stop, selling gasoline and diesel. In 1955, Knecht sold the station and moved a few blocks to the east, where he built a 2,000-square-foot truck parts store and stocked it with $10,000 worth of inventory left over from the previous business. The store sat on the same five-acre parcel where Knecht was raising his family.

The traditional auto parts industry frowned on Knecht's unorthodox business practices of catering to do-it-yourself mechanics initially. But the concept would eventually form the backbone of a successful chain.

Auto parts stores in the 1950s sold their product to dealers and professional installers, who would serve the public.

Knecht sold directly to the public for the same price, bucking tradition and setting the stage for what would become the modern-day auto parts retailer.

Nate's son Wally joined the company in 1962 and helped Knecht's take retail to a new level.

Wally set up a retail outlet inside Mark's Big M Shopping Center near downtown Springfield. The shopping center itself was located within the building Booth-Kelly Co. originally constructed just after the turn of the century to house Springfield's first sawmill.

Neither the shopping center nor the auto parts outlet was successful, but Knecht's pressed forward. In 1967, Wally opened a retail store on Highway 99 in Eugene. A third store opened the following year. By 1975, the Knecht's chain included six stores.

Knecht's formed an affiliated company, KAPCO United Inc., in the mid-1970s. KAPCO's warehouse and offices are located adjacent to the original Knecht's auto parts store on Main Street.

KAPCO serves as the central distribution center and merchandise purchasing location for all Knecht's outlets. It also functions as a control center to manage pricing, advertising and daily operations.

Wally's daughter Karrie Cutsforth runs KAPCO distribution center. Other loyal employees and a third generation of Knechts help keep the business running smoothly. Wally's nephew Greg Knecht joined the company in 1985 to open stores in Salem and Portland. Jeff Knecht, Greg's brother, works with Greg. Dave Powell and Dave Weleber both have served the company since the early 1960s. Kevin Sabbato, Wally's son-in-law, also is a new partner in the company. He works in the Bend area.

Knecht's has grown steadily over the years. It operates 22 outlets in Oregon, including seven in Lane County, two of which are in Springfield. Knecht's employs 235 workers throughout the state, including 102 in Lane County.

Wally Knecht expects his company to continue its growth into the next century. *◗*

MACHINIST WOODWORKERS
LOCAL LODGE W246

BOOTH KELLY WOODS

Springfield's two most prominent labor unions began serving workers locally in the late 1930s, fighting for family wage jobs, a safer work place, and job security.

The union known today as Machinist Woodworkers Local Lodge W246 received its first charter in 1937. At its inception, the union was part of the International Woodworkers of America, one of the earliest affiliates of the Congress of Industrial Organizations (CIO).

Names changed over the years as unions merged.

Today, the union represents 300 Springfield members who work primarily at Willamette Industries Trucking and the particleboard and plyveneer portions of Weyerhaeuser Co.

Another active Springfield labor union—the Western Council Industrial Workers Local 2750—was chartered

in 1941 with 300 members. Local 2787 received its first charter in 1945, and local 3035 followed two years later.

Today, Local 2750 represents 345 working members and 80 retirees. Local 2787 represented 285 plywood workers at Springfield Plywood, formerly Georgia-Pacific. Local 3035 represented Clear Fir Products door plant, formerly known as Morgan-Nicolia. All the members from these locals were merged into 2750.

In the immediate post-war era, the high rate of union-ization among wood products workers made Oregon the sixth most heavily organized state in the country.

Local labor agreements set high standards for wages, hours, and working conditions. Springfield's unions represented dozens of smaller companies with 50-60 employees, as well as the large manufacturers.

The 1950s ushered in the heyday of labor unions in Springfield. During the next two decades, unions organized in just about every trade.

Labor unions represented movie houses, restaurants, barber shops, almost all logging operations, and dozens of other trades.

The union's influence on wages, benefits, and working conditions routinely reached into non-union shops. Once union's negotiated contracts for their workers, non-union employers often were quick to follow suit with changes in wages and benefit packages mirroring the new union contracts. Union leaders say that still happens today within the industries they serve.

Times changed in the 1970s and 1980s. Larger mills had bought out most of the smaller operations, and union membership waned due to technological change, competition from Canadian lumber, and dwindling timber supply.

The Springfield membership in the Machinist Woodworkers Local W246 fell from 2,800 in 1978 to 300 in 1985.

The wages and benefits enjoyed by Springfield wood products workers were the result of great sacrifices by members of the IWA and WCIW. At least two major strikes occurred (in 1953 and 1986) and one lockout by the employers in 1963.

Today's Machinist Woodworkers union is part of Machinist International (IAM & AW), AFL-CIO, which represents 600,000 workers nationwide. The Western Council is affiliated with the United Brotherhood of Carpenters of America, AFL-CIO, another union of 600,000.

Today, Springfield's labor unions continue their long tradition of serving hard-working members and ensuring a fair, safe, and prosperous working environment. ❶

NORM'S AUTO REPAIR, INC.

Sometimes times don't really change all that much. Case in point, Norm's Auto Repair, Inc., 112 Main Street, just off the Willamette River's eastern banks, was a good location for an auto repair shop in 1928. Seventy years of progress haven't changed it.

Norm Dahlquist's classic small business opened in 1928 as Thurman's Service Station.

O.C. Thurman owned and operated a feed store on the site until state officials condemned the structure so they could extend Main Street across the river into Glenwood.

Thurman built a gas station on the site.

John McGinty bought the business around 1940 and hired C.B. "Punk" Dunnington to run the station. Dunnington later bought the business.

Norm's father, Bud Dahlquist, came to work for Dunnington in 1946 as a mechanic.

Bud Dahlquist left the shop in 1959 to open Mohawk Texaco with a partner in January 1960.

Almost exactly a year later, Dahlquist sold his portion of Mohawk Texaco and bought the Main Street Texaco.

Norm Dahlquist joined his father at Dahlquist Texaco in 1972. Bud retired in the late 1970s and Norm ran the business. Norm actually purchased the shop in January 1981.

The longtime service station stopped pumping gas in 1988, when new Department of Environmental Quality standards prompted Dahlquist to remove his underground storage tanks.

Dahlquist served on the city of Springfield's Budget Committee for six years and was elected to a four-year term on the City Council. He served from January 1995-99.

Cars and the methods for repairing them have changed significantly in the past 70 years. But much has remained the same at 112 Main Street It always was the right place for a small auto repair shop. ❧

O.C. Thurman in front of the original Norm's Auto Repair, Inc. Little change was made until the 1940's.

BORDEN CHEMICAL INC.

Borden Chemical Inc. constructed its Springfield resin plant in 1946 and began production at the facility two years later. The company built its first West Coast site in Springfield in an effort to grow with the post World War II population out west. New York-based Casein Company of America, a division of Borden, originally operated the plant to manufacture synthetic resins for the plywood industry.

Over the years, the plant expanded its manufacturing capabilities to serve a broader range of forest products companies. Today the plant makes resins for particleboard, laminated beam, and melamine (decorative furniture) in addition to the plywood resin. It also produces formaldehyde, the base ingredient for the resins.

Kolberg, Kravits and Roberts bought out Borden's parent Company in 1994. The Springfield plant main-

tained its original name through the ownership change.

The facility currently employs 110 workers, including sales, research, and development staffs at its 15-acre site. Borden serves the local wood products industry primarily. The company also ships some resins worldwide, usually for testing purposes.

Company managers expect the plant to continue its traditional operations well into the future. The company will soon extend into its third century.

Gail Borden Jr. formed Borden Inc. in New York in 1857. Gail Borden invented Eagle Brand condensed milk, which remains one of the most popular brands on the market today. ❧

MODERNE BRIGGS STUDIO

For more than four decades, the words "Moderne Briggs Studios" stamped on a photograph has meant quality. And the talent behind the viewfinder was Jack Briggs—Photographer, adventurer, and father.

Jack Briggs was raised around the rolling hills of Sheridan, but by the early 1940s, he was in the midst of World War II, serving as a counter-intelligence agent working as a photographer and darkroom technician for the U.S. Army.

One of his most memorable assignments was in Hiroshima, Japan, soon after the United States dropped the H-bomb. Surviving the war years, in 1947 Jack moved to Springfield with his wife Catherine. Using his photographic skills, the Briggs soon began to make a name for themselves taking pictures at local nightclubs and social events.

In 1950 Jack opened Moderne Photography and Camera Shop on Main Street and became involved in local politics. He was elected to Springfield City Council in 1954, serving one term. Still attracted to adventure, Jack was one of the original investors in Springcraft Boats in 1957. The boat business eventually sunk, but Moderne Studios prospered, moving to its current location on North A Street.

When not taking senior portraits or shooting family reunions, Jack dabbled in motion pictures; from under the ice in Antarctica, to sharks in the warm waters of the South Pacific.

Moderne Studio expanded to Eugene in 1985, opening a studio on the corner of 13th and Oak streets. Photographing families, high school seniors, and Kidsports, Moderne is known throughout the state of Oregon for its great school photos, dances, and senior portraits.

The company started with Jack and Catherine as the total work force and has grown locally to employ Harold and John Briggs (owners) and approximately 25 to 30 people, producing all its own photographs here in Springfield—remaining a family business striving to produce quality portraits at affordable prices for the past 50 years.

Although Jack died of cancer on January 31, 1995, his sons, Harold and John, and daughter Mary, keep the photography business alive. ◑

OREGON INDUSTRIAL LUMBER PRODUCTS, INC.

Oregon Industrial Lumber Products, Inc. still fulfills the potential founder Al Clements saw in Springfield's timber industry in 1948.

Clements, a former Georgia Pacific forester, purchased 12 acres of land along Marcola Road and built an 86,000-square-foot plant.

Originally known as Al Clements Lumber Co., the business initially employed 30-35 workers.

The company purchased rough green clear lumber from mills throughout the Northwest.

Workers kiln dried the lumber, surfaced, and packaged it, then sold it to customers nationwide.

The company has remained close to its roots for the past 50 years while expanding its horizons.

Oregon Industrial Lumber as it looked in the early 1950s.

Today, Oregon Industrial Lumber Products, Inc. processes Douglas fir into specialty lumber products and ships them throughout the United States, Canada, Asia, and Europe.

Two brothers, Douglas and Grant Orme, purchased the plant in 1968. W. Verne McGuire bought an interest in 1971.

McQuire and Douglas Orme became the sole owners when Grant retired two years later.

Current owner Murray McDowell bought a one-third interest in the company in 1983 and acquired the outstanding shares four years later.

Oregon Industrial currently employs 50 workers. The company makes mouldings, flooring, and other specialty products.

"There are a few people who do some of the things we do. But nobody does all of what we do," McDowell said.

A solid market niche, a cooperative city government, and Springfield's historically healthy balance between business and environmental interests all have combined to make Oregon Industrial Lumber Products, Inc. successful for a half-century. ◑

Ebbert Memorial United Methodist Church is noted for its 23 stained glass windows. Photo courtesy of Camdon Draeger, Moderne Studios.

Chapter Ten

1951 TO PRESENT

DOUBLETREE HOTEL

Eugene Mayor, Jim Torrey(left), and Lane County Commissioner Steve Cornacchia enjoy a chocolate chip cookie on the opening day at Doubletree Hotel.

Located just off Interstate 5, the 12,000-square-foot Doubletree Hotel—with its 234 guest rooms, seven suites, and spacious meeting and convention facilities—is the nucleus of a thriving retail and recreation district in Springfield.

In fact, the Gateway area—including the Gateway Mall—was literally built around Doubletree Hotel, which was first constructed in 1973 by Jim McClory as a Rodeway Inn. The 151-room unit, complete with swimming pool, putting green, and tennis courts opened December 20, 1973.

Just a stop off the freeway at that time, the hotel (or "motor inn" as it was then called) sat surrounded by cornfields. In the early 1970s, there were only 80 guest rooms in the local area. By the late 1990s there were 1,150—the largest concentration of rooms in a six-block area between Seattle and San Francisco. (The Doubletree Hotel is currently the third largest hotel in Lane County and the largest in Springfield.)

In 1979, Red Lion Hotels and Inns purchased the Rodeway Inn, and along with becoming a premier hotel, the Red Lion became a favorite nightspot for locals, as well as out-of-town guests.

After another switch of owners, Doubletree Hotel came into existence in 1997, merging with Red Lion Inns and creating a new identity for the hotel virtually overnight.

"It was June 9, 1997," said John Erickson, who has been managing the hotel since 1988. "It really was quite a day. All the signage, pens, light switches, letterheads, 135 nametags—everything had to be converted from Red Lion to Doubletree in one day. Guests went to sleep in a Red Lion Inn and woke up in a Doubletree Hotel."

Creating a comfortable and cozy atmosphere is a company goal. Guests are treated to amenities such as free parking, mail and package handling, and fax capability, but what Doubletree has become famous for is its fresh baked chocolate chip cookies, given to every guest upon check-in.

"People underestimate the cookies, but they're a powerful thing," Erickson said. "They are baked right here, more than 500 cookies a day, which is 180,000 cookies a year. Along with giving them to guests, we also take them when we go out into the community."

But Doubletree Hotel gives more than just cookies back to the community.

The organization is well-known for its generosity and supports many programs, such as the Start Making a Reader Today (SMART) literacy program, United Way, and the Make-A-Wish Foundation.

Other involvement includes the Thurston Healing Fund (which came in the wake of the May 1998 shootings at Thurston High School), Rotary Youth Cup Soccer, and the Rotary Duck Race.

"We developed a care committee and we are very involved in community service," Erickson said. "Doubletree's philosophy is that participation in the community is vital to the company's success."

Management is also interested in the issue of room tax. Currently, Lane County has a guest room tax, and a portion of this goes back into the city of Springfield, supporting youth programs, Fire and Life Safety, and tourism.

The hotel regularly holds customer appreciation events, such as inviting customers to tailgaters at University of Oregon football games and other appreciation events.

In addition, for more than two decades, the University of Oregon Ducks football team members and their coaches stay at the hotel before every home game, staying overnight and partaking in a huge buffet breakfast the next morning.

Erickson said along with developing and improving customer service, Doubletree Hotel is committed to its employees.

"We work at increasing employee morale and have many incentive programs," he said. One of those is a once-a-month "Mystery Guest" program, where one guest is given lodging, food, and phone calls free in exchange for an honest evaluation of service.

"Even the front desk doesn't know in advance," Erickson said, "and I only find out when the report crosses my desk."

He said the program is an excellent way to discover areas of needed improvement, but also showcases "star employees."

Although the hotel is one of more than 1,250 company hotels in the United States and Mexico, it stays true to its commitment of connection to the community.

For example, Doubletree Hotel is a charter member of the Springfield Filbert Festival, an annual arts, music, and cultural festival held in Island Park on the banks of the Willamette River every summer.

With 12 separate meeting rooms and a ballroom large enough to serve 1,400 people, Doubletree Hotel is well suited to serve as host to many local events, including the annual Mayor's Prayer Breakfast and the Mayor's Ball. Only 15 minutes from the Eugene Airport, with complimentary transportation, the hotel continues to be a convention and conference destination for business and industry.

Along with full-service, customized catering, Doubletree Hotel offers guests complete in-house audio-visual equipment and built-in public address systems.

Guests can keep in shape at the hotel's health club, tennis courts, spa, or heated outdoor pool. In addition, several golf courses, bike paths, and jogging trails are minutes away. Opportunities for rock climbing, river rafting, hiking, and skiing are also nearby.

Other commodities include the Doubletree Lounge, which offers nightly entertainment and dancing; The Grill, which specializes in sizzling steaks, seafood, and pasta; and conveniently casual all-day dining at the Coffee Garden.

Nearby attractions include the Dorris Filbert Ranch, Springfield Museum, the McKenzie and Willamette Rivers, vineyards, and the Hult Center for the Performing Arts.

From its early years as a solitary motor inn sitting in the middle of farmland, to the first-class amenities it offers today, the Doubletree Hotel has remained an important cornerstone in the development of Springfield. ❶

Doubletree Hotel.

One of Doubletree's spacious banquet rooms.

MCKENZIE-WILLAMETTE HOSPITAL

*(above) Early
fund-raising
breakfast.*

*Opening Day
at the hospital.*

McKenzie-Willamette Hospital was truly built as a labor of love by the residents of Springfield to improve the community's health and quality of life.

Although a handful of private physicians had practices in their residences, in the mid-1940s the growing city had no hospital to call its own.

The former Springfield Private Hospital had been converted into a boarding house in 1914, replaced by Springfield General Hospital, which was converted into apartments in 1936. And due to flooding in the Glenwood area, reaching the hospital in Eugene was virtually impossible at times.

By 1949, a group of determined residents began seriously discussing the possibility of building a full-service hospital in Springfield and formed the McKenzie-Willamette Hospital Association. Little did they realize that their dream would take root and flourish into a multimillion dollar, modern health care campus less than 50 years later.

Through old-fashioned fund-raising—which included scrambled egg breakfast meetings and door-to-door pleas from mothers pushing babies in their carriages—a group of about 150 volunteers made it possible to purchase a parcel of land at 14th and G Streets in July 1953.

A victory banquet October 30, 1953 celebrated $480,000 in pledges and payments from more than 3,500 individuals businesses and civic groups, as well as $155,000 in federal funds.

With Harry Wright serving as the hospital's first chairman of the board, the doors of McKenzie-Willamette Hospital opened on Sunday, May 1, 1955, with almost 3,000 residents attending the dedication ceremonies of the new 35-bed facility. A proud moment came in October 1956 when the Joint Commission on Accreditation of Hospitals granted the hospital full accreditation.

The hospital continued to grow through the 1960s. The East Wing was completed in 1961, adding 19 beds to the existing 35. In 1964, an emergency department, expanded operating room, and recovery room were added, followed in 1968 by new business offices, physical therapy, laboratory, and expanded radiology departments, and in 1969, an intensive care unit.

By the 1970s, the number of patients had increased to the point that patients' beds were sometimes seen in the corridors due to overcrowded wards. Other problems included scheduling the two operating rooms.

After discussion, the board of directors announced a long-range expansion plan with a $4.5-million first-phase construction program. Again, the residents of Springfield and surrounding communities came through by pledging $532,000 in 1973. The money was used to build a four-story addition which would house new operating rooms, a recovery room, central supply, medical records, purchasing, larger dietary facilities, a storeroom, and a 36-bed nursing unit, bringing the total number of beds to 104.

In the 1980s, the hospital again outgrew its facilities,

and the community responded with $1.1 million in contributions. A new 72,000-square-foot ancillary building was opened in October 1983, housing diagnostic services, full-body scanning, a 14-bed intensive care and coronary care unit, and a short-stay center. In addition, the hospital installed a helicopter landing pad on the roof, allowing a patient to be transported to a Portland hospital in 45 minutes.

Hospital reorganization in 1987 led to specialized areas of health care, called "Centers of Excellence," which included Senior Services, Occupational Health, Women's Services, and Preventative Services.

In 1991, McKenzie-Willamette Hospital became the first hospital in the state to receive full Level II trauma status—the highest trauma designation awarded to a nonteaching hospital.

Keeping affordable patient care in the forefront, in 1993 the hospital and more than 150 physicians formed a partnership to provide services and comprehensive health care under the name McKenzie Health Care.

Also in 1993, the hospital foundation initiated the annual Festival of Trees, which has raised more than $1 million. That same year, the hospital became affiliated with Planetree, a patient-centered philosophy that led to changes in ambience, such as colorful uniforms and fresh baked goods in the Intensive Care Unit. An important part of Planetree was the idea that if patients have access to information, they can help to restore their own health—both during their hospital stay and at home. It is a philosophy of personalizing, humanizing, and demystifying care. (The hospital is no longer officially affiliated with Planetree but continues to encompass a similar philosophy in patient care.)

The late 1990s included construction and completion of the Jack V. Fuller Guest House, Adult Day and Health Care Center, and the Women's Health and Birth Center.

The 114-bed hospital also serves as a training center for Health Occupations Students of America from both Springfield and Thurston High Schools, and at any one time, more than 100 volunteer members of the McKenzie-Willamette Hospital Auxiliary provide services such as delivery of food trays, mail, and flowers, as well as emotional support to patients.

Looking beyond the 1990s, McKenzie-Willamette Hospital's President and Chief Executive Officer, Roy J. Orr, said, "At McKenzie-Willamette Hospital, the history of community support and individual contributions is unlike any I have ever experienced. Over the years, this intense level of participation has been the single greatest reason for McKenzie-Willamette's continued success.

During the 1970s and 1980s, many hospitals organized into large systems, often spanning several states. Such systems sometimes distracted hospital management from responding to community needs. During those same decades, however, McKenzie-Williamette remained an independent organization whose sole purpose was to listen to—and serve—the community's health care needs.

As a community-owned, secular hospital, all decisions regarding strategic direction are made right here by a community-based, 15-member board of directors. Since MWH is a nonprofit hospital, income and assets are reinvested into top-quality medical services, equipment, and employee benefits.

Looking to the future, the board of directors and administrative leadership will continue to assess the community's health care needs based on advice from patients, local citizens, and community leaders. As health care practices constantly advance, much of its effort will focus on prevention and wellness.

McKenzie-Willamette's essential purpose is the same as it was in 1955: "We are committed to changes that keep up with advances in medicine, while at the same time respecting our heritage of community support and participation. As our mission statement says, we are 'People dedicated to improving our community's health and quality of life.'" ✿

Emergency Services entrance.

SONY DISC MANUFACTURING

If the rainbows weren't enough, a committee member who is an avid golfer found a golf ball buried halfway in the ground while walking through an orchard on the property. The nearest golf course is five miles west.

Other more practical factors would soon convince Sony to build in Springfield.

Local leaders were waiting with open arms and a modern economic development plan designed to attract their first major high-tech employer in Springfield's history.

Years before Sony came calling, Lane County leaders recognized the need to diversify the economy.

The timber industry that had dominated the economy for decades could no longer sustain the area as it had for so long.

Leaders saw Sony as the centerpiece to those vital economic diversification plans.

Sony bought 120 acres of orchards and farmland. Springfield worked overtime to streamline its building application process.

The partnership allowed Sony to finish its $50-million, 336,000-square-foot facility in one year.

Former Oregon Gov. Barbara Roberts helped the New York-based company break ground for the facility on May 10, 1994.

Springfield leaders hailed Sony's arrival as a major coup and an example of how planning and cooperation could lead Lane County away from its traditional dependence on timber.

Pilot production began exactly one year later. It came more than three months ahead of schedule and was the fastest start-up in company history. In addition, the company received ISO 9000 and 14000 series certification, an internationally recognized standard, for its manufacturing and environmental quality systems.

Double rainbows arcing over the picturesque Coburg Hills greeted a group of Sony Corp. employees as they flew over the Willamette Valley in 1993.

It would prove an ominous sign of good things to come.

Sony's site selection committee was searching for an ideal location for a new West Coast disc manufacturing facility.

Managers at the New York-based company decided in the early 1990s that they needed a facility out west. Sony believed the West Coast offered untapped potential in the optical disc industry. A plant out west would allow the company to better serve its varied group of customers.

The committee scoured Nevada, Arizona, Oregon, and parts of California for the perfect location. Their visits to Springfield always seemed to bring a sign that they had found the right spot.

Springfield's plant is Sony's fourth prerecorded digital media production facility in the United States.

Sony quickly began to reciprocate Springfield's warm welcome.

The company worked closely with Lane Community College in nearby Eugene to develop a job training program.

Local residents, many of whom were displaced workers from the timber industry's downturn, learned the skills necessary to earn family wage incomes at Sony.

The partnership resulted in Sony's hiring 92 percent of its current 400-employee workforce from within Oregon and more than 75 percent from Lane County.

"A key to our success in starting up this new facility has been the quality of this Oregonian workforce," said Thomas Costabile, senior vice president, operations.

Workers use state-of-the-art technology to reach a capacity of about 12 million audio CDs, CD-Rom, and Sony PlayStation™ discs per month. The plant operates 24 hours per day, seven days per week.

The Springfield plant helps make Sony the world's largest optical disc manufacturer. It is one of seven facilities in the Americas, including those in Toronto, Rio de Janeiro, and Mexico City.

Sony built the United States' first compact disc plant—Digital Audio Disc Corporation—in Terre Haute, Indiana, in 1983.

Since then, the corporation has consistently led the industry into new frontiers.

In 1986, Sony introduced CD-ROM (Compact Disc Read Only Memory). The new technology combined music and audio with video, still pictures, graphics, and text. It offered customers an entirely new interactive multimedia experience.

The Sony PlayStation™ game platform followed in September 1995 and quickly became one of the world's most popular game formats.

Sony continues to play a key role in the introduction of new high-density optical disc technologies, such as DVD, and recently added a Digital Authoring Services unit to its Springfield plant operations.

In the local community, Sony plays an active role in supporting United Way social services, education, and the arts. An employee committee recommends opportunities for company sponsorship and encourages other employees to get involved by volunteering their time to local causes.

Sony also partnered with local radio stations to recognize and encourage the innovative use of technology in education.

One of many examples includes a program the company helped foster at Thurston High School. Students, with help from Sony representatives and other community volunteers, worked for nine months developing a CD-ROM program that provided a guide to the modern high school experience. Sony pressed the program onto a CD-ROM disc, allowing Thurston to market the product.

Sony also helped other local high school students create an innovative multimedia project outlining Springfield High School's long history.

Part of Sony's long-range plans involves establishing a high-tech campus-like setting surrounding its plant.

The 120 acres located just off Interstate 5 with the Coburg Hills in the background offer Sony plenty of space for future expansion. Last September, Sony, via a joint venture, opened a 6,600-square-foot child development center on an acre parcel just across International Way from the plant.

Sony leased the property to a private company that owns and operates the day care facility.

Part of Sony's employee benefit package includes a partial tuition waiver for their children to attend the day care and preschool.

"A total employee benefits package that includes child development is an important factor in a company's ability to recruit talented individuals," according to Noreen Franz-Hovis, director of human resources for Sony's Springfield plant.

Employees sitting in the plant cafeteria can see the day care center about 150 yards away. Sony's collaborative effort to provide quality day care is part of a new trend many other large Oregon employers currently are considering. ❂

COMFORT FLOW HEATING

For Richard Schoolcraft, owner of Comfort Flow Heating, the company's Springfield location was love at first sight, or perhaps "site."

More than two decades before the company moved to its current home in the Springfield Industrial Park, Schoolcraft saw the site along recently completed I-105 while he was driving back to Eugene from a job in Springfield.

"I noticed this piece of property from the freeway in 1971," Schoolcraft said from his West Springfield office, which overlooks lush, emerald green, tree-lined hills to the south and east. "I thought, 'What a great place to have the business!' "

But it would be several years before Schoolcraft's dream materialized into the elegant, yet comfortable office complex—what he calls his "home away from home"—that houses Comfort Flow Heating today.

The company's story begins in 1961, when former owner Don Lahmers established the name "Comfort Flow." In July of 1964, Lahmers sold the company to a 23-year-old Schoolcraft, who had been a Comfort Flow employee.

Comfort Flow's first office was in a tiny warehouse off Second Street in Eugene with about a half-dozen employees and the same number of vehicles. For a short period of time, the company was in a warehouse

on Franklin Boulevard in Glenwood, then in December 1969, Schoolcraft purchased a site on West First Street in Eugene that had previously been the location of Brighter Homes Electric.

In the early years, Comfort Flow employees worked mostly with residential builders installing heating systems, such as natural gas forced air furnaces.

At that time, very few people in the local area were installing air conditioning units—and heat pumps were almost unheard of. In the 1970s, as natural gas rates went from 18 cents to more than 60 cents a therm (a therm equals 100,000 B.T.U., or British thermal units, of heat), and electricity went from 8/10 of a cent to almost 5 cents a kW (kilowatt), Comfort Flow began looking for more efficient systems to install.

Due to government mandate in the 1980s, homes were made more energy efficient and, as they were built tighter, indoor air quality became a concern as well. Gas furnaces, with their higher combustion efficiency (also mandated by the government), and the amazingly efficient heat pumps became very popular with homeowners.

Unfortunately, the increased insulation that keeps houses comfortably warm in the winter also makes them uncomfortably hot in the summer and early fall, leading to more requests for air conditioning systems. Houses and buildings that don't lose heat in the winter also won't lose it in the summer.

Through the years, as some residential builders evolved and began doing more commercial work, Comfort Flow grew with them installing heating, ventilation and air conditioning (HVAC) systems in restaurants, shopping malls, and office complexes.

By the mid-1990s, Comfort Flow had outgrown its

Eugene location. Schoolcraft began searching for new sites and was excited to learn the Springfield Industrial Park land was still available. Having worked for builders and developers for more than 30 years and being a licensed contractor himself, Schoolcraft designed the building and developed the property that is now Comfort Flow's central office. In September 1995, Comfort Flow moved into its current location, just off I-105 in the Springfield Industrial Park.

Today, the company employs more than 75 workers, who install and repair HVAC systems in both business and residences throughout Oregon.

The family tradition of honing new skills is continuing with Schoolcraft's son, Trieber Meador, who is currently learning the business from the ground up.

In addition to their ongoing residential work, notable Comfort Flow commercial projects include HVAC work at the new Springfield branch of SELCO Credit Union on Harlow Road, Springfield Goodwill, Springfield Family Practice, Cascade Fabrication, Berean Assembly of God Church, and the Gateway branch of South Umpqua Bank; Monaco Motorhomes and Marathon Coach in Coburg; as well as Riverfront Research Park and the Ed Moshofsky Sports Center near the University of Oregon's Autzen Stadium, in Eugene. Other recent projects include FOOD for Lane County, the Downtown Athletic Club in Eugene, and Lane County Fairgrounds.

One of the non-monetary rewards of running an apprenticeship-based company, Schoolcraft says, is watching young men and women learn valuable blue-collar skills.

"The skills they learn are transferable," Schoolcraft says. "These skills will stay with them and benefit them anywhere they may go allowing them to earn family-wage jobs for the rest of their lives."

In fact, after working for the company for several years, two Comfort Flow employees recently retired.

Although Comfort Flow has evolved and grown through the years, quality is still a number one priority. The company continues to provide affordable and efficient heating, ventilation, and air conditioning systems in homes and businesses throughout Oregon.

In addition, customer service does not end with sales. Comfort Flow employees monitor systems and provide service and repairs for customers long after installation is completed.

Whether providing service, repair, and installation for private residences—or for a large, multi-faceted commercial projects—Comfort Flow has kept its customers' needs as its central focus for more than 35 years.

As energy needs change in the future, Comfort Flow will be there. Always on the cutting edge, Comfort Flow will be installing more energy efficient—and always environmentally friendly—systems. ◗

CENTENNIAL BANK

This is how Centennial Bank in Springfield looks today.

The merger led to an expansion of the board of directors and the naming of a new president, Richard C. "Dick" Williams. In the early 1990s, administrative offices were moved from Springfield to the new four-story Centennial Bank building in downtown Eugene. In 1992, *Forbes* magazine rated Centennial as one of the top 10 small banks in the country.

As Centennial Bank continues to grow, senior management is challenged to keep its original focus on friendly, personalized service. From the top down, everyone is committed to the task of serving customers with a community bank style. All employees— including loan officers and branch managers—are expected to provide teller services if lobby traffic demands it. At the same time, there is a commitment to provide expanded services to take advantage of increasing resources. By Dec. 31, 1998, Centennial Bank had grown to well over one-half billion dollars in assets, with 14 branches from Cottage Grove to Portland.

Community involvement remains important. Two of the Springfield Chamber of Commerce presidents since 1974 have been Centennial Bank officers, and bank personnel have been active leaders in service clubs, numerous local nonprofit organizations, fund-raisers, and committees.

The bank credits its loyal friends, customers, and shareholders who are the "heart" of continued success, and while it's come a long way from its modest beginnings, Centennial Bank will not forget Springfield is its cradle. ◑

In the mid-1970s advertisements for the newly formed Centennial Bank invited local residents to "Come share our heart-to-heart banking—and let's grow together in our town."

Centennial Bank was conceived in the early 1970s by a group of Springfield-area businessmen who felt local banks were getting too big and impersonal during an era of "merger mania." Wanting to create a bank that was smaller and more community oriented, their brainchild was realized with formal regulatory approval in December 1973.

Founders included Chairman Robert S. Cochran and board members Daren C. Engel, William E. Fitch, Miles McKay, Donald D. Derickson, and Clifton G. Christian; as well as President C. L. "Tek" Haugen and Senior Vice President Ron R. Peery.

Groundbreaking for the 5,600-square-foot, brick building—designed by architect James Keefe and constructed by Ordell Construction—began in the Mohawk area in early 1974.

Meanwhile, on Jan. 10, 1974, "Springfield's Own New Bank with Young Ideas" opened for business in its temporary headquarters (a mobile home on the southeast corner of M Street and Mohawk Boulevard) with six employees and assets of about $750,000.

From its infancy, Centennial Bank has operated with a mission statement featuring a unique twin objective: Provide growth and earnings to its shareholders by serving the financial needs of businesses and individuals through excellent, personalized service.

By the time of ribbon cutting for the new building on May 9, 1974, deposits had already exceeded the $2-million mark.

In September 1981, shareholders approved a merger with Eugene-based Valley State Bank. On April 1, 1982, the merger was complete, sending Centennial on its way to being the largest independent bank in Oregon.

Two early employees at Centennial Bank's first location at the southeast corner of M Street and Mohawk Boulevard.

LANE COMMUNITY COLLEGE

Although the main campus of Lane Community College is nestled in the hills of southeast Eugene, it has a long history with Springfield.

In 1959, Springfield High School Principal Dale Parnell began searching for something that would serve as a bridge for students between high school and university.

That something was a community college.

Parnell went on to become superintendent for the Lane Intermediate Education District (now Lane ESD), and he was able to advocate for formation of the Lane County Community College Study Committee.

In March 1964, Bert Dotson, who had taught vocational courses and was dean of boys at Springfield High School, was hired by the committee to manage a campaign to obtain voter approval for a new college and to oversee preliminary organization of the college.

On Oct. 19, 1964, Lane County residents voted Lane Community College into existence.

Elected to the charter Board of Education were Albert Brauer, Clifford Matson, Kenneth Schmidt, Dean Webb, William Bristow, Jr., and at-large members Olga Freeman and Lyle Swetland. Schmidt represented Zone 3, which includes the Springfield and Marcola school districts.

In its first year, Lane enrolled 1,500 students in 13 state-approved vocational programs, adult education, and college transfer classes. For the first three years, classes were held in nearly four dozen locations throughout the district, including Springfield.

"I remember when we taught all over," said Delpha "Debbie" Daggett, health teacher, in an October 1994 interview with *The Springfield News*. "We were known as the 'Monroe Street Gang' or the 'Bethel Group.' I taught health in the old Georgia-Pacific building at Fourth and D Streets in Springfield and remember timing my lectures according to the train schedules."

In March 1965, college officials selected a permanent campus after industrialist Wilfred Gonyea donated a 100-acre tract of land in southeast Eugene. The board accepted the free acreage and purchased an additional 48.81 acres in August 1967.

The college moved its main campus to the 30th Avenue location in September 1968.

The college curriculum continually diversified to fit the needs of its students. In the 1970s, when an increasing number of women wanted to go to school to return to the workforce, the Women's Center developed a women's reentry class. A similar program, called Transitions to Success, with a Displaced Homemakers component, exists today. In the 1980s, when the county saw massive layoffs from the timber industry, Lane created a

Dislocated Workers Program, which became a model for similar programs throughout the country. The college also added a Business Development Center and a Business and Industry Services Department to help employers train employees.

STARTech was a preemployment training program developed by Lane's Training and Development Department in partnership with Sony Corporation's disc manufacturing center in Springfield and Symantec Corporation in Eugene. The program offered training in computers and communications for possible employment in high-tech industries between 1995-98.

In May 1995, voters approved $42.8 million in bonds to expand and improve existing college facilities and to create community learning centers at eight high schools.

On Dec. 8, 1997, the 3,300-square-foot Lane Community College Learning Center at Thurston High School opened, featuring a 24-workstation computer lab to be used by high school and Lane students, as well as the community.

By 1998-99, Lane Community College was serving more than 37,000 students throughout its 5,000-square-mile service district.

With its pioneer learning center programs, President Jerry Moskus says the college is not just a place on the hill, "but a part of the community."

"Lane is staying true to its vision of 'providing quality learning experiences in a caring environment,'" he says. ❶

Classroom in Springfield, March 1966.

Georgia-Pacific Building, 1965.

DORMAN CONSTRUCTION INC.

In less than a decade, Steve Dorman has taken Dorman Construction Inc. from its humble beginnings in a small bungalow on 37th Street in east Springfield to a multimillion-dollar company.

In 1990, while working as vice president for a local contractor, Steve Dorman and his wife, Suzy, decided to sell their 5,000-square-foot dream home and use the profits for seed money to begin their own construction firm.

They moved into a 960-square-foot rental house, using one bedroom as "the office."

"I remember I took the metal doors off the closet and stuck my computer and fax machine in there," Steve Dorman said in November 1998. "When I began, I didn't have a single employee or one job lined up."

However, Dorman, who had been in the construction profession for years, didn't have to wait long. Almost immediately he was asked to repair roof trusses at South Eugene High School in Eugene. He did the work alone, but soon a former coworker, Mark Miller, asked if he could join Dorman.

Miller, as Dorman's first official employee, still carries the nickname "Number One."

Together, the men began bidding successfully on local jobs. The number of employees grew to nearly a dozen in the first year. By 1992, they had outgrown the little house on 37th Street and moved into an office on Q Street in Springfield. In the first two years, Dorman Construction surpassed nearly $12 million in sales, and in three years, the company had completed more than 100 projects.

The business continued to flourish, and in March 1995 the office was moved to its current 1.5-acre site in Coburg Industrial Park, off Interstate 5.

Dorman Construction now has 50 employees, and Suzy Dorman serves as the secretary and treasurer.

One of the company's most impressive feats is the King Estate Vineyards Winery in Lorane. Their work earned honors with the Oregon Concrete and Aggregate Producers Association.

Other notable ventures include remodels and continuing projects at both Sacred Heart Medical Center in Eugene and McKenzie-Willamette Hospital in Springfield; renovations at Springfield's Booth-Kelly complex; a 22,000-square-foot classroom and gymnasium addition at Mohawk High School

in Marcola; a fleet maintenance facility for the City of Springfield, and a $2-million renovation for Lebanon Community Hospital. The company has also subcontracted concrete work for Knight Library at the University of Oregon, a new Lane County Juvenile Justice Center, and a new FOOD for Lane County facility. In its first 10 years, the company completed projects worth $300 million.

Recently, Dorman Construction added custom mausoleum design and construction to its repertoire, and has sent crews to Ohio, Oklahoma, Georgia, and Virginia.

Steve Dorman, owner and president of Dorman Construction Inc., is a 1971 graduate of Springfield High School, and although he now owns homes in both Eugene and in Pennsylvania, his roots are in Springfield.

"I grew up on 16th and 17th Streets," he said. "Although we work all over, I feel we'll always have strong ties to Springfield." ❂

SANIPAC INC.

In the early 1970s, about a dozen small haulers joined forces to begin a garbage service for local residents. Along with Springfield Sanitary Service, that early group was the precursor of Sanipac Inc., Lane County's largest garbage collection and recycling service.

Facilities were moved from 28th Street, and later Enid Road in Springfield, to off Airport Road northwest of Eugene.

By 1977, Sanipac Inc. had moved to its current Glenwood location near the Lane County Solid Waste Transfer site.

In 1980, the Pape' family purchased Sanipac Inc., and by the mid-1980s, garbage collection included recycling services. Around the same time, Sanipac Inc. began using automated trucks. The days of a person lifting and dumping cans into a truck were over—at least on the trash side of things.

Recycling still requires hand sorting. Adding a little whimsy to their workload, the company developed its "Recycle Zoo" program in 1984 to educate the public on the value of recycling. Characters such as "cardvark-boardus corrugatas" and "cangaroo-cannus flatinus" are used to elicit interest in the young—and young at heart.

"We knew that if we wanted recycling to work, we'd need to aim it at the kids," says Sanipac Inc. General Manager John Hire. "When I was a kid, the big thing was littering. Our parents were taught not to throw things out the window of the car. Today's kids know about recycling. If they see a tin can in the trash, they'll call their parents on it. Recycling needs to be ingrained in the kids. That's our goal."

In the early years, recycled goods were picked up every other week, but in May 1990 Sanipac Inc. announced weekly service and every customer received a blue plastic recycling box in addition to their trash can. Curbside recycling grew from 1 million pounds in 1990 to 25 million pounds in 1998.

As residential recycling grew, so did the commercial and industrial recycling. To accommodate, Sanipac Inc. built a 52-thousand-square-foot Material Recovery Facility (commonly called a "merf," for MRF) in May 1996. The $5-million EcoSort facility, also located in Glenwood, enables Sanipac Inc. to sort through and recycle up to 35 percent of the waste, from commercial and industrial, as well as construction customers.

In 1998 the company had about 4,000 commercial and 39,000 residential accounts across Lane County. Sanipac Inc. serves Springfield exclusively through a contract with the city.

Hire said drivers now visit up to 7,500 homes twice a day, once for garbage and once for recycling, which means almost four million times a year, one of 75 vehicles comes to a person's home.

With 125 employees, the company's administrative offices will move to a larger facility adjacent to its current Glenwood building in June 1999.

The future will bring more changes, and since Sanipac Inc. has always stayed "ahead of the curve," those changes will come to Springfield.

"And the bottom line is," Hire says, "no matter how much things change, we'll still be out there every day to pick up your garbage." ✿

B & I TRUE VALUE

B & I Plumbing and Electric was opened by Carl Gardner and Bill Beedon in 1970 as a branch of a Tacoma-based company.

Originally located at 3875 Main St., B & I specialized in basic plumbing and electrical supply. During a deep recession in 1983, Robert and Jean Frachiseur purchased the company.

Jobs were scarce and the Frachiseurs had considered looking out of state to find work. They ultimately chose to remain in Springfield.

"We decided there wasn't a better place to raise our kids," Robert says. Robert brought 25 years of plumbing and electrical experience to the company, which thrived during the 1980s by providing local do-it-yourself homeowners and contractors with materials for home construction and repair.

With business booming, B & I soon outgrew its location. In 1988, it was moved to a more spacious store about five blocks east on Main Street. With more room to grow and with increasing competition from large home center stores, Robert and Jean decided to join the True Value co-op.

Since True Value is the world's largest hardware buying group, it enabled the Frachiseurs to increase their inventory lines and continue to offer competitive prices.

B & I became a full hardware retailer adding product lines such as paint, tools, and hardware while increasing the company's existing plumbing and electrical departments.

In 1997, B & I had again outgrown its location. Robert and Jean moved the store to its current location at the 5700 block of Main Street in the fast growing Thurston area.

The store's workforce increased over the years along with its size and inventory.

When Robert and Jean first purchased B & I, the store employed two workers. Today, the workforce has reached 24.

"Our employees are what makes B & I successful. Their knowledge and customer service is why we are open for business," Robert says.

In October 1998, the True Value co-op relocated a main warehouse from Portland to Springfield. As a result, B & I receives 75 percent of its merchandise locally in Springfield.

"We try to do as much business as possible locally to keep our money in the community," Robert says.

Over the years, B & I has contributed to numerous civic projects in the community, such as joining with the Springfield Rotary Club to light Hamlin Field.

Robert and Jean feel it is important to contribute and be involved with a community that has been good to B & I and the Frachiseur family. ◑

ROMANIA ENTERPRISES

For more than three decades, the Romania name has been synonymous with automobile sales and service to the people of Springfield, Eugene, and greater Lane County.

Moreover, Steve Romania, president of Romania Enterprises, said he sees that trend continuing well into the new millennium and beyond.

"Our goal is to stay in the same geographic area and stay in the car business as a privately owned business for years to come," he said.

The Romania story started in the early 1940s, when Joe Romania (Steve's father) began selling tires and auto accessories in a Billings, Montana, department store. After the war, Joe began selling tires at the local Sears, Roebuck & Co. store, but he soon moved from tire sales to car sales, working for Lew Williams Chevrolet, also in Billings.

Joe moved west in 1957 when his boss bought the Silva Chevrolet dealership in Eugene (near Glenwood) and offered Joe a 25 percent partnership in the new Lew Williams Chevrolet. By 1969, Joe had completed buyout of the dealership and bought his own sign: "Joe Romania Chevrolet."

Steve Romania grew up in the business watching his father. He spent summers as a teenager sorting nuts and bolts in the parts department, eventually moving into sales positions. By the time he graduated from the University of Oregon in 1976, Steve was ready to combine a lifetime of hands-on learning with a new business degree and apply it to the family business.

Although the mid-1970s (up to 1978) were good sales years, the 1979 oil crisis and sharp rise in import sales pointed the Romanias towards diversification.

In 1982, the company tapped into a regional— and even national—sales market by adding recreational vehicle sales and service. A separate RV facility, established in 1983, was moved to its current Highway 99 location in 1992.

Aiming for the growing import market, Steve, along with his wife Lori, opened the Hyundai dealership in Eugene in 1989. Romania Imported Motors bought out Vic Alfonso Toyota in 1992 and merged into Romania Chevrolet, Inc. to create one of the top 50 private companies in Oregon.

That same year, Steve Romania was named president, taking over for his father, Joe, who retired.

In 1998, along with owning Chevrolet, Hyundai, Toyota, and Subaru dealerships, the company added "Romania's Used Cars & Trucks" in west Eugene.

A member of both the Springfield and Eugene Chambers of Commerce, Steve Romania is proud to be a longtime employer in the area, with many 30-year-plus employees.

Along with its customers, the Romania name is familiar to fans who look up at the scoreboard in Mac Court during University of Oregon Duck basketball games.

Along with sponsoring the scoreboard since 1969, the company has provided vehicles for various coaches and helped raise funds for Autzen Stadium.

Steve Romania said the company will continue to offer new and used cars and service to customers in the Springfield and Eugene area for many years.

"We plan on sticking around a long time," he said. ✪

Joe and Steve Romania.

The showroom of Romania Chevrolet in earlier years.

GLOBE METALLURGICAL INC.

The silicon smelter started production in Springfield on January 4, 1954, as a single furnace operation. APEX Smelting Co. built the plant to produce silicon for the Pacific Northwest aluminum industry. Since then, the plant has changed ownership numerous times, yet always responded to challenges in a demanding industry.

Silicon is produced by reducing quartz rock in a submerged electric-arc furnace.

The availability of low-cost hydroelectric power was a main factor in attracting the company to Springfield.

In 1959, the plant started a second, larger furnace to increase production. American Metal Climax purchased the plant in 1962 and upgraded both furnaces to increase production.

Kawecki Berylco Industries bought the plant in 1967 and named it National Metallurgical.

In 1975, the company installed a third furnace. The larger new furnace had a higher production output than the other two combined. The company shut the other two down within the next two years.

Cabot Corp. bought the plant in 1978 and sold it to Dow Corning Corporation in late 1980.

Dow Corning upgraded the facility's plant emission systems and removed the two old furnaces. The plant's new mission was to produce silicon for the silicone chemical market and serve as a research facility.

Globe Metallurgical purchased the 12.5-acre facility in July 1993. Globe brought with it a rich history within the ferro-alloy industry. The company originally formed in 1873 as Globe Iron Co. and is believed to have produced iron for the *Merrimac* shielding.

The *Merrimac* was the first ironclad warship and fought the Union Monitor to a stalemate during the Civil War.

Globe Metallurgical Inc. formed in 1987. Today, it is the nation's largest silicon producer and ranks second in the world.

The company received national recognition in 1988, when it won the first Malcolm Baldridge National Quality Award for small business.

President Ronald Reagan presented the award to Globe CEO Arden Sims.

Globe's Springfield plant markets silicon to both the silicone chemical and aluminum industries.

More than 2,500 commercially available products contain material made with silicon.

Silicon produced in Springfield is found in aluminum car parts, adhesives and bathtub caulks, personal care products such as deodorants and shampoos, lubricants, polishes, water repellents, and paints. The products also are used in the aircraft and aerospace industries and as food additives in potato chips and Coca-Cola.

The silicon produced in Springfield can be converted into the silicon chips found in computers and into products such as exterior tiles used on space shuttles.

Globe Metallurgical's 43 employees look forward to the plant's 50th anniversary in 2004. The company continues to grow, with operations in Alabama, Ohio, New York, England, and Norway as well as Springfield.

Globe employees accept the Globe motto "The Challenge Never Ends." Through teamwork, the employees make the Springfield plant a model for the industry. ❶

purchase and renovation of the mall in 1979. After completion, the City authorized the Historical Commission to use the power station as a museum for a trial period of five years.

The Historical Commission created a Museum Committee to staff the museum early in 1980. Original members were Dick Lasater (director), Noel Dean Van Dyke, Chris Larson, Linda Kay Emory, Arlene Joranger, Myrnie Daut, Barbara Stockwell, Barbara Abrams, Ellen Miller-Wolfe, Alicia Nott, Graydon Lewis, Edwin Kinsley, Bonnie Denning, Dorothy Snelling, and Beth Trudgeon.

By 1992, the Museum formed a board of directors which began a capital campaign to build the Historic Springfield Interpretive Center, located in the second floor gallery. The total estimated cost was $225,000. The group raised funds by contacting members of the community, as well as conducting a "Buy a Brick" campaign in 1995.

The Interpretive Center opened in February 1996, the only exhibit of its kind in Lane County.

Currently, the Museum Committee works with a full-time director, Kathy Jensen, who is employed by the City of Springfield. Committee members help schedule exhibits, work on collection care and cataloging, do the buying and display for the Museum Store, and plan special events.

The Museum averages 10,000 visitors annually and offers 10 rotating exhibits of art and historic collections in its Main Street Gallery.

With the building itself an architectural treasure in the community, the Springfield Museum continues its history of "serving as a historical and cultural center for the citizens of Springfield." ❶

While sharing local history with its patrons through exhibits, the location of the Springfield Museum itself is notable—listed on the National Register of Historic Places.

Both the Museum and the Historic Springfield Interpretive Center upstairs are housed in the former Oregon Power Company Building, built in 1911.

The Museum first opened its doors in September of 1981 with an exhibit on the hops industry, which had flourished in the local area from 1887-1937. It began as a nonprofit, all-volunteer venture with the mission of "serving as a historical and cultural center for the citizens of Springfield, promoting community pride and identity through the development of historical and cultural resources, as an outreach center, for displays, exhibits, lectures, workshops, drama, music, dance, and other arts as they relate to the citizens and the heritage of the City."

The concept of a city museum began in the 1950s with a group of Pioneer Club members who were worried local history wasn't being preserved. The group began gathering artifacts and information. They secured a place in the school district's Administration Building on Mill Street in the late 1970s, but later had to move.

The museum idea resurfaced in August 1977 when the City of Springfield and the Chamber of Commerce created the Historical Commission. In 1979, the City of Springfield investigated the purchase of the old Spring Village Shopping Mall for use as City Hall. Part of the mall property included the old brick substation, which was vacated by Pacific, Power, and Light in 1976. First slated for demolition, the building was rescued as a result of public interest in its preservation and possible use for a museum. Citizens passed a ballot measure authorizing

MONACO COACH CORPORATION

670,000-square-foot motorized facility in Wakarusa, Indiana.

The new plant allowed Monaco to consolidate all Indiana motorized production under one roof with plenty of room for expansion into new model introductions.

As a result, all towable production was consolidated at Monaco's existing Elkhart, Indiana facilities.

Monaco opened a new Springfield manufacturing facility in 1997. The plant introduced McKenzie, a new line of towable RVs developed primarily for the West Coast market.

The company plans additional significant expansions in Oregon in the near future.

A project to provide additional manufacturing capacity on a 37.5-acre lot adjacent to their current Coburg facility is targeted for completion in late summer 1999. It will add 525,000 square feet of facilities used to build both Monaco and Holiday Rambler brand motorhomes.

Today, Monaco Coach Corporation is the nation's fourth largest RV manufacturer and continues to gain ground on the top three.

Monaco employs 3,000 workers in Coburg, Springfield, and three sites in Indiana.

The company helps get customers involved in clubs and rallies and offers publications and top-notch after-sale service.

Monaco's common stock is listed on the New York Stock Exchange under the symbol *MNC*. ◐

Monaco Coach Corporation arose from modest beginnings to become an industry-leading highline RV manufacturer.

As the successor to a company originally formed in 1968, Monaco has experienced some turbulent times.

Kay L. Toolson joined Monaco in 1986. Former Eugene mayor, Brian Obie's diversified Obie Industries, owned the company at the time.

Toolson and his management team kept the company moving forward through some lean transitional years.

In March 1993, Toolson bought the company's assets and operations. Monaco completed an initial public stock offering the same year.

Toolson moved Monaco in late 1995 from a 25-year-old plant in Junction City to a new 300,000-square-foot facility in Coburg. The move helped the company increase weekly production by 66 percent.

Monaco completed a few small acquisitions between 1987 and 1995 that helped the company grow.

The most significant acquisition came in March 1996 when Monaco acquired Holiday Rambler Corporation, the RV division of Harley Davidson. Holiday Rambler was one of the nation's leading manufacturers of medium-priced recreational vehicles.

In 1997, Monaco continued its expansion and consolidation plans by completing its new state-of-the-art,

PSC INC.

Consumers most commonly recognize PSC Inc. products during trips to the grocery store as they watch the clerk quickly scan their purchase items for the price with a machine that reads the information off an attached product bar code.

PSC Inc. is a worldwide leader in the bar code, retail automation, and automatic data collection industries.

Formed in 1969 in Rochester, New York, the company manufactures the world's most comprehensive line of laser-based hand-held bar code readers, on-counter retail checkout scanners, and related products.

PSC products are used for efficient automatic data collection in the retail, manufacturing, transportation, and distribution industries.

Health care providers and government agencies also use the products.

From its infancy, PSC has pioneered new technology in the data capture industry. In 1992, PSC's acquired organization, Spectra-Physics, became the industry's first company to become ISO 9001-certified.

The company expanded its market coverage substantially in 1996 by acquiring the Data Capture Group of Sweden-based Spectra-Physics, including US-based Spectra-Physics Scanning Systems, Inc.

Spectra-Physics—originally a division of a California-based company—built a 54,000-square-foot facility in west Eugene in 1979. A 56,000-square-foot facility was added in 1985. The facility serves as PSC Inc.'s key manufacturing site today.

Spectra-Physics designed the first retail bar code scanner and installed it in an Ohio supermarket chain in 1974.

During the next two decades, Spectra-Physics grew into the world's leading supplier of fixed-position bar code scanners for a variety of retail point-of-sale applications.

Spectra-Physics's flagship product, the Magellan 360-degree scanner-scale, sets an industry standard for grocery and mass merchandise stores.

PSC continues to lead the industry with a new generation of innovative products, including the U-Scan Express self-checkout system, the first customer operated checkout system of its kind.

Other state-of-the-art PSC products include "Direct Illumination" bar code reading engines that measure only 1.2 cubic inches without compromising reading performance. It is billed as the world's smallest point-of-sale scanner.

The company produces high-speed unattended scanners to serve a rapidly growing demand for automated materials and sorting applications.

PSC also is a world leader in bar code verification technology, which tests all major coding systems. ●

GOOD NEIGHBOR
CARE CENTERS, L.L.C.

Good Neighbor Care Centers, L.L.C. began as a labor of love.

In 1985, while seeking an appropriate care facility for his father, Brent Hedberg realized there was a need for something different, and the seed for a new type of care center was planted.

After a year of intense research and several meetings between founders and board members—Brent Hedberg, Bill and Cherie Wheatley, and Dan Desler—the decision was made to proceed with plans for a community-based care facility of individual, homelike dwellings in a campus-type, residential setting.

Good Neighbor Care Centers, Inc. was incorporated in 1987, and was formed to meet the growing need for quality, affordable, long-term care as an alternative for people who would otherwise be placed in an institutional setting, such as an intermediate nursing home.

The first home, Max Parrott, was opened in 1987. Although Brent Hedberg died in 1988 and new owners came on board, the company continued to grow, opening two more homes in Springfield.

The Board of Directors, realizing the company's rapid growth, initiated the company's first Human Resource Audit, which resulted in many hours of training, and the ultimate implementation of team management, core competencies, purpose, and vision.

The company is committed to training and educating employees, as well as providing them with outstanding benefits. Both the management and the care-giving style are unique, using a Horizontal Management model that allows employees to have a voice in the decision-making process.

When Good Neighbor Care Centers, L.L.C. first opened, they had three employees. Now, in the late 1990s, the company has nearly 90 employees in nine homes in Springfield specifically serving the needs of persons with Alzheimer's disease, other forms of dementia, and mental health issues.

Good Neighbor Care Centers, L.L.C. also contracts with Lane County Mental Health and the State of Oregon to provide care in a "Passages Home."

In addition to permanent resident placement, Good Neighbor provides Day and Respite Care services.

The corporate officers include Dan Desler, Shareholder-Director, Chairman and Chief Executive Officer; David McCurdy, President and

Shareholder-Director; and Cherie Wheatley, Shareholder-Director and Chief Operating Officer.

Both Dan Desler and Cherie Wheatley are active in the Oregon Health Care Association, as well as numerous civic organizations. Dan Desler serves on the Oregon State Medicaid Long-term Care Quality and Reimbursement Council, the Legislative Issues Committee of the Springfield Chamber of Commerce, and is a sponsor for Boy Scouts of America. Cherie Wheatley's community involvement includes association with the Eugene Rotary, the Relief Nursery, the Association of Junior Leagues, and the Symphony Guild.

Since its inception more than a decade ago, Good Neighbor Care Centers, L.L.C. has continued to be a caring community for those who need assistance with daily living.

Looking toward to the new millennium, Good Neighbor Care Centers, L.L.C. is poised to begin expansion with plans to develop 55 new projects over the next five years. Each project will consist of five 15-bed specially designed homes for the care of people with Alzheimer's disease and dementia. Expansion is targeted to take place in the Western United States in the fall of 1999. ♦

APAZ ARCHITECTS, AIA

Long before most architects recognized its importance, Artemio Paz Jr. incorporated innovative energy concepts into aesthetic building designs.

Those concepts emerged in the mid-1970s when Paz became a partner in Rosenberg and Paz, AIA. In the Pacific First Federal Building, Paz used daylighting with skylights and south-facing windows to produce an expansive two-story building with heavily landscaped indoor planting.

Artemio Paz, Architects, AIA was formed in 1975. Paz's projects continued to emphasize traditional usage of solar space heating and daylighting. HUD awarded Paz a financial grant to design a passive solar heated residence, in 1979. The following year, Paz used passive solar heating in designing Springfield Fire Station 4, which was recognized nationally and in the Northwest as unique. While maintaining his Springfield office, Paz taught architecture at his alma mater, the University of Oregon.

Later, Paz extended his innovative design approach to include public and institutional projects, such as The Torrance Performing Arts Theater and the Carlsbad Public Safety buildings in California. His designs helped create the UO Chiles Business Center with its popular raised courtyard entrance, the Eugene Station Square Building, and McKenzie-Willamette Hospital's new zoning district.

APAZ is currently assisting the Springfield Renaissance Development Corporation with its design to revitalize Springfield's downtown urban core. This plan emphasizes small public spaces, waterway restoration and mixed use housing activities with a focus on environmental and sustainable design criteria. ❂

ECONO SALES, INC.

Econo Sales, Inc. gathers merchandise from across the nation, draws customers from throughout the Northwest, and reaches into Africa's poorest communities.

For Springfield residents, the company's unusual product line has been no further than a walk downtown for more than 30 years.

Joe and Helen Beaver opened Econo Sales in 1966, filling the showroom at 326 Main Street with damaged freight and wholesale liquidation type merchandise.

Econo Sales later evolved into a business selling material for upholstery, along with drapery fabric and supplies.

Bill Beaver bought the business from his parents in 1981 and moved it to more spacious accommodations next door at 330 Main Street the following year.

When Beaver passed away in 1991, he left the store to longtime employee Maria Myott and her husband, Larry.

Today, Econo Sales sports the region's largest selection of upholstery fabric. "We draw customers from all over the Northwest," Maria Myott said.

Maria scours the United States looking for new fabric lines. "When I took over, we had a dozen cotton prints. Now we have more than 400," Myott said.

A doctor visits the store once each year and garners 18 yards of muslin, a lightweight cotton fabric, which he gives to babies he cares for during visits to poor villages in Africa.

In many cases, it's the only clothing the baby has, Myott said.

Econo Sales has remained loyal to downtown Springfield even after shopping malls began to dominate the retail scene in Lane County. ❂

REALTY WORLD-HARLOW

For local Realtor Artie Mae Harlow, Springfield is home—as well as a place to sell homes. After more than three decades in the realty business, she is "still selling Springfield and loving it!"

Artie Mae and her husband Bob have two sons, Robert and Dennis. Harlow Realty was founded in September 1965. With a focus on Springfield and East Lane County properties, the Harlow's ran their company with the idea that "Every home is a castle to somebody."

By July 1975, the sales staff had grown from four to 16, and the office was moved from Deerhorn Road to its current site at 1510 Mohawk Boulevard.

Her professional and energetic attitude has led to many honors, including serving as president of the

Artie Mae Harlow

Eugene-Springfield Multiple Listing Service and the Springfield Board of Realtors and being chosen Springfield's Realtor of the year—twice. She also assisted the state's Real Estate Agency and the Oregon Association of Realtors in revising real estate licensing laws, and she worked with the department of Housing and Urban Development and Federal Housing Authority on rules for property disposition.

Although busy with her profession, through the years Artie Mae has found ways to give back to the community—through helping establish the Springfield Teen Center, membership in the Thurston High School Swim Team Booster Club, raising money for McKenzie-Willamette Hospital, and participating in a monthly, multi-church sing-a-long.

Volunteerism has been hereditary in the Harlow family for four generations. One of Artie Mae and Bob's sons, Dennis Harlow, a sales manager and agent at Realty World-Harlow, is a volunteer coach for local youth sports programs.

Although Artie Mae purchased the Realty World franchise in September 1996, the company remains family owned and operated. Since its beginnings, the company's focus has been commitment to its customers. As the sales team says, "We are all 'sold' on the Springfield area!" ♦

ZILKOSKI AUTO ELECTRIC

The dream that eventually became Zilkoski Auto Electric began in the 1930s when Bill Zilkoski worked with his brother in an auto electric shop.

In 1953, Bill and a partner first opened Economy Garage. In 1962, Bill bought out his partner and renamed the business Zilkoski Auto Electric and opened a new shop on the same site on North 39th Street.

Zilkoski's son-in-law, Arlen Kopperud, began working at the shop in 1965. Kopperud bought half the business in 1972.

During those years, Bill's wife and co-owner, Leona, served as secretary and receptionist and continued in that capacity for many years. Bill passed away in 1973.

The growing business built a new 6,000-square-foot facility in 1975 next to the outgrown former shop.

Kopperud and his wife, Marceil Kopperud, bought the business outright in 1979. The company currently employs 10 trained auto electricians and an office manager.

Zilkoski Auto Electric has always specialized in testing, diagnosis, repair, and replacement of anything related to electrical systems.

The company services all models of cars, trucks, RVs, boats, and other types of equipment that operate with electrical systems.

Zilkoski's also rebuilds starters, generators, and alternators, provides expert wiring and rewiring services, and stocks a full line of batteries and other electrical parts.

Bill's dream remains a reality at Zilkoski Auto Electric, where the staff skillfully handles today's technology and prepares to meet tomorrow's challenges.

His two grandsons, Keith and Aaron, appear to carry on the legacy. Both currently are employed in the company. ♦

INTERCITY INC.

Intercity Inc. is the tale of a business that lies between two cities—Springfield and Eugene.

The Glenwood firm, which now designs, develops, and manufactures electronic equipment, has deep roots in the local area.

The original Intercity company was founded in the mid-1920s when "Sig" Moe purchased an interest in Springfield Sand and Gravel and ran the business out of an office at Mill and South B streets in Springfield.

In 1929, Moe moved the company to its current location. The original two-story office, built with leftover bridge timbers, looks south over the family home on Franklin Boulevard.

Through the 1940s-1960s, Intercity Sand and Gravel helped build the streets, sewer systems, and bridges of most of Springfield.

In 1960, Moe sold out the sand and gravel company and focused on the construction side of things, using the name Intercity Construction. The company, with about 50 employees, stayed intact until 1971.

At that time, Sig's son, Steve Moe, took over the family's business name creating Intercity Inc., a research, manufacturing, and development firm. One of his first designs and patents was a radio controlled traffic control

system used at construction sites.

Today, Intercity Inc.'s employees design, develop, and manufacture electronic equipment, controls and circuit boards for clients such as Country Coach, a recreational vehicle company, and the U.S. Forest Service. Many of the company's designs, such as a timer-based air pollution monitoring system, are used around the world.

Steve Moe is committed to local communities through his involvement on the boards of the Glenwood Water District, the Springfield Filbert Festival, and the Lane County Planning Commission.

Through the decades, Intercity Inc. has remained an important business partner in the Springfield and Glenwood area. ✪

LANE TRANSIT DISTRICT

More than a century before mention of mass transit, public transportation was prevalent in Springfield with the river ferry, "Echo," owned and operated by the McCully family of Harrisburg. By 1910, streetcar service between Eugene and Springfield was added, but by 1927, automobile use and extensive public funding of new roads caused its demise.

That year, the city councils of Eugene and Springfield approved a franchise request by the streetcar service's owner, the Southern Pacific Company, to replace the streetcars with motor buses. A succession of private companies operated the bus system with varying degrees of success for the next three decades, but by the late

1960s, the owners announced that they would discontinue service due to declining revenues.

It was then that the cities of Eugene and Springfield petitioned then-Governor Tom McCall to create a mass transit district for the area. In 1969, legislation was passed and Lane Transit District, or LTD, was born.

Through the years, LTD has consistently ranked among the top five medium-sized transit systems in the United States. In 1985, LTD became one of the first transit systems in the nation to be 100 percent wheelchair accessible. Along with group bus pass programs, LTD operates highly popular park and ride shuttle services to the Springfield Filbert Festival, the Lane County Fair, and University of Oregon basketball and football games.

Today, LTD employs more than 300 local citizens and transports six million passengers a year. Thousands of Springfield residents ride LTD every day. In fact, the No. 11 Thurston bus route has long been LTD's number one route in total ridership.

In the near future, a proposed Bus Rapid Transit pilot corridor will extend from east Springfield, to Glenwood, continuing LTD's long history of providing efficient and reliable service to its customers. ✪

NESTE RESINS CORPORATION

Neste Resins Corporation, a supplier of resins for the wood products and industrial building products industry, has been a major employer in Springfield for nearly four decades.

Founded in 1960 by a group of men with previous experience in the adhesives industry, Central Processing Company (as it was then known) was built at the site of a former potato chip factory in east Springfield. Most commonly known as Chembond, the plant became Neste Resins in 1990. Neste Resins Corporation is wholly owned by Neste OYJ, the Finnish national oil company.

As a supplier for the wood products industry, Neste Resins has diversified through the years to meet the needs of its customers. The company uses a team approach between its research and development, sales, technical service, and plant workers.

Although Neste Resins is part of a worldwide operation, its importance to the local wood products industry can't be underestimated. Through well-established contracts with major global producers (which assures reliable supply and quality) and long-term relationships with local customers, Neste Resins has remained an important part of Springfield's economy for nearly 40 years.

Neste Resins is committed to a clean, safe, and healthy environment and to train, equip, and direct its employees to perform their jobs in a safe and environmentally responsible manner. It is important to the company to be a major contributor to the community through donations, involvement, and care. It is proud to be an important part of Springfield's future, as well as its history. ❶

Aerial view of Neste Resins.

Most of the homes in the Washburne Historic District are smaller than this structure, originally a home and now a law office. Photo courtesy of Camdon Draeger, Moderne Studios.

EVERGREEN LAND TITLE COMPANY

Evergreen Land Title Company was licensed February 13, 1981 by Scott Stovall and Jessie Fountain.

The company's reputation for excellence and reliability was established through close business relationships with its early customers, such as Daren Engel Real Estate, Red Carpet Real Estate, Artie Mae Harlow of Harlow Realty, Naslund & Armstrong Attorneys, and the City of Springfield.

Evergreen Land Title was the first title company in the country to develop software to research title company records, and that software is now used in several hundred installations throughout the United States.

Priding itself on innovation, the company strives to proactively approach situations before they become problematic.

The name Evergreen Land Title Company is now connected to several large projects, such as the Gateway Mall and McKenzie-Willamette Hospital in Springfield, and Hyundai Semiconductor in west Eugene.

Evergreen Land Title Company also prides itself on community involvement. For example, owner and cofounder Scott Stovall served on the Springfield Utility Board of Directors from 1988-1994.

"Evergreen aspires to be a responsible—and responsive—'corporate citizen,'" Stovall says, "We work at channeling our financial and personnel resources back into the community that made us what we are."

From four employees in 1981, to nearly 40 employees today, Evergreen Land Title Company continues to provide title insurance services, escrow closings, and title plant construction; keeping the needs of not only its customers—but also the communities it serves—close to its heart. ❂

Smith Mountjoy riding his pride and joy, an Indian motorcycle, in 1913. Photo courtesy of the Springfield Museum.

SPRINGFIELD ENTERPRISE INDEX

APAZ Architects, AIA
86590 Cedar Flat Road
Springfield, Oregon 97478
Phone: 541-744-2046
Fax: 541-744-1017
E-mail: apaz@clipper.net
page 149

B&I True Value
5790 Main Street
Springfield, Oregon 97478
Phone: 541-747-6101
Fax: 541-747-4019
E-mail: bitruevalu@aol.com
www.truevalue.com
page 142

Borden Chemical Inc.
470 South 2nd Street
Springfield, Oregon 97477
page 125

Brandt Finance Company
806-A North A Street
PO Box 1352
Springfield, Oregon 97477
Phone: 541-746-2543
Fax: 541-746-8223
E-mail: bfsi@teleport.com
page 121

Centennial Bank
1377 Mohawk Boulevard
PO Box W
Springfield, Oregon 97477
Phone: 541-726-8111
Fax: 541-726-2768
www.centennialbancorp.com
page 138

City of Springfield
225 5th Street
Springfield, Oregon 97477
Phone: 541-726-3700
Fax: 541-726-2363
E-mail: rpryor@ci.springfield.or.us
page 96

Comfort Flow Heating
1951 Don Street
Springfield, Oregon 97477
Phone: 541-726-0100
Fax: 541-726-4799
E-mail: cflow@cmc.net
pages 136-137

Dorman Construction Inc.
32986 Roberts Court
Coburg, Oregon 97408
Phone: 541-984-0012
Fax: 541-984-0013
www.dorman-const.com
page 140

DoubleTree Hotel
3280 Gateway Street
Springfield, Oregon 97477
Phone: 541-726-8181
Fax: 541-747-1866
E-mail: dbltree@cyber-dyne.com
www.doubletreeeugene.com
pages 130-131

Econo Sales, Inc.
330 Main Street
Springfield, Oregon 97477
Phone: 541-746-5003
Fax: 541-741-4666
www.econosales.com
page 149

Evergreen Land Title Company
1570 Mohawk Boulevard
Springfield, Oregon
260 East 11th Avenue
Eugene, Oregon
Phone: 541-741-1981
Fax: 541-741-0619
E-mail: scott@evergreenlandtitle.com
www.evergreenlandtitle.com
page 153

Globe Metallurgical Inc.
1801 Aster Street
Springfield, Oregon 97477
Phone: 541-746-7674
Fax: 541-736-3598
page 144

Good Neighbor Care Centers, L.L.C.
622 South 57th Place
Springfield, Oregon 97478
Phone: 541-747-3373
Fax: 541-747-0673
E-mail: cwheatley@goodneighbor.com
page 148

Intercity Inc.
3698 Franklin Boulevard
P.O. Box 847
Springfield, Oregon
Phone: 541-726-7613
Fax: 541-747-7516
E-mail: intercity@aol.com
page 151

Knecht's Auto Parts
3400 Main Street
Springfield, Oregon
Phone: 541-746-4532
Fax: 541-746-0884
E-mail: knechts@teleport.com
www.knechts.com
page 123

Lane Community College
4000 East 30th Avenue
Eugene, Oregon 97405
Phone: 541-747-4501
www.lanecc.edu
page 139

Lane County
125 East 8th Avenue
Eugene, Oregon 97401
Phone: 541-682-4203
Fax: 541-682-4616
www.co.lane.or.us
page 98

Lane Transit District
PO Box 7070
Eugene, Oregon 97401
Phone: 541-682-6100
Fax: 541-682-6111
E-mail: ltd@ltd.lane.or.us
www.ltd.org
page 151

**Machinist Woodworkers
Local Lodge W246**
1116 South A Street
Springfield, Oregon 97477
Phon: 541-746-2541
page 124

Marshall's Inc.
4110 Olympic Street
Springfield, Oregon 97478
Phone: 541-747-7445, 541-461-4444
Fax: 541-741-0821
page 119

McDonald Candy Co.
2350 West Broadway
Eugene, Oregon 97402
Phone: 541-345-8421
Fax: 541-345-7146
page 102

McKenzie-Willamette Hospital
1460 G Street
Springfield, Oregon 97477
Phone: 541-726-4400
Fax: 541-744-8565
E-mail: kaybry@mckweb.com
www.mckweb.com
pages 132-133

Moderne Briggs Studio
656 North "A" Street
Springfield, Oregon 97477
Phone: 541-746-4438
Fax: 541-746-4439
www.modernestudio.com
page 126

Monaco Coach Corporation
91320 Industrial Way
Coburg, Oregon 97408
Phone: 541-686-8011
Fax: 541-681-8899
www.monaco-online.com
page 146

Myrmo & Sons, Inc.
3600 Franklin Boulevard
Eugene, Oregon 97403
Phone: 541-747-4565
Fax: 541-747-6832
page 99

Neste Resins Corporation
475 North 28th Street
Springfield, oregon 97477
Phone: 541-746-6501
Fax: 541-746-6273
www.neste.com
page 152

Norm's Auto Repair, Inc.
112 Main Street
Springfield, Oregon 97477
Phone: 541-747-2002
Fax: 541-747-4471
E-mail: normd@efn.org
page 125

**Oregon Industrial Lumber
Products, Inc.**
PO Box 1442
Springfield, Oregon 97477
Phone: 541-746-2531
Fax: 541-746-4483
page 126

154 *Springfield*

PSC Inc.
959 Terry Street
Eugene, Oregon 97402
Phone: 541-683-5700
Fax: 541-687-7982
E-mail: eujobs@pscnet.com
www.pscnet.com
page 147

Realty World-Harlow
1510 Mohawk Boulevard
Springfield, Oregon 97477
Phone: 541-746-4060
Fax: 541-746-1225
E-mail: harlow.realty@harlows.net
www.harlows.net
page 150

Reed's Fuel & Trucking
4080 Commercial Avenue
Springfield, Oregon 97478
Phone: 541-746-6535
Fax: 541-746-4585
pages 108-111

Romania Enterprises
1410 Orchard Street
Eugene, Oregon 97403
Phone: 541-465-3232
Fax: 541-343-7107
E-mail: sromy@aol.com
www.romaniadealerships.com
page 143

Rosboro Lumber Company
PO Box 20
Springfield, Oregon 97477-0086
Phone: 541-746-8411
Fax: 541-726-8919
www.rosboro.com
pages 112-113

SaniPac Inc.
1650 Glenwood Boulevard
Eugene, Oregon 97403
Phone: 541-747-2121
Fax: 541-747-5958
www.sanipac.com
page 141

Sony Disc Manufacturing
123 International Way
Springfield, Oregon 97477
Phone: 541-988-8000
Fax: 541-988-8099
http://sdm.sony.com
pages 134-135

**Springfield Area Chamber
of Commerce**
101 South A Street
PO Box 155
Springfield, Oregon 97477
Phone: 541-746-1651
Fax: 541-726-4727
E-mail: general@springfield-
chamber.org
www.springfield-chamber.org
pages 106-107

Springfield Museum
225 5th Street
Springfield, Oregon 97477
Phone: 541-726-3677
Fax: 541-726-3689
E-mail: kjensen@ci.springfield.or.us
page 145

The Springfield News
1887 Laura Street
Springfield, Oregon 97477
Phone: 541-746-1671
Fax: 541-746-0633
E-mail: thenews@rio.com
www.springfieldnews.com
page 99

Springfield School District
525 Mill Street
Springfield, Oregon 97477
Phone: 541-747-3331
E-mail: pr@sps.lane.edu
www.sps.lane.edu
page 97

Springfield Quarry Rock Products
800 South 18th Street
Springfield, Oregon 97477
Phone: 541-747-1213
Fax: 541-747-7266
pages 114-115

Springfield Utility Board
PO Box 300
250 A Street
Springfield, Oregon 97477
Phones: 541-746-8451
Fax: 541-746-0230
www.subutil.com
page 122

Square Deal Lumber
Phone: 541-746-2576
Fax: 541-746-2579
E-mail: squaredeallumber@msn.com
page 120

Timber Products Company
PO Box 269
305 South 4th Street
Springfield, Oregon 97477
Phone: 541-744-4227
Fax: 541-744-5431
E-mail: lhartwig@teamtp.com
www.timberproducts.com
page 100

University of Oregon
Public Affairs and Development
1270 University of Oregon
Eugene, Oregon 97403-1270
Phone: 541-346-5555
Fax: 541-346-0499
E-mail: uopad@darkwing.uoregon.edu
www.uoregon.edu
page 101

**University of Oregon
Alumni Association**
1204 University of Oregon
Eugene, Oregon 97403-1204
Phone: 541-346-5656
Fax: 541-346-2822
alumni@oregon.uoregon.edu
http://alumni.uoregon.edu
page 101

Washington Mutual Bank
North Springfield
650 Q Street
Thurston
5703 Main Street
Phone: 800-756-8000
page 100

Western Bank
3545 Gateway Street
Springfield, Oregon 97477
Phone: 541-726-2800
Fax: 541-744-9624
page 100

Weyerhaeuser
PO Box 275
Springfield, Oregon 97477
Phone: 541-746-2511
Fax: 541-741-5343
www.weyerhaeuser.com
pages 92-95

Wildish companies
PO Box 7428
3600 Wildish Lane
Eugene, Oregon 97401
Phone: 541-485-1700
Fax: 541-683-7722
www.wildish.com
pages 116-117

**Willamalane Park
& Recreation District**
200 South Mill Street
Springfield, Oregon 97477-7303
Phone: 541-736-4044
Fax: 541-736-4025
E-mail: mail@willamalane.org
www.willamalane.org
page 118

Zilkoski Auto Electric
200 North 39th Street
Springfield, Oregon 97477
Phone: 541-747-9213
Fax: 541-746-8641
page 150

BIBLIOGRAPHY

American Institute of Architects, Southwestern Oregon Chapter. *Style and Vernacular: A Guide to the Architecture of Lane County, Oregon*. Portland, OR: Oregon Historical Society, 1983.

Applegate, Shannon. *Skookum, An Oregon Pioneer Family's History and Lore*. New York: Quill William Morrow, 1988.

Beckham, Steven Dow. *The Indians of Western Oregon*. Coos Bay, OR: Arago Books, 1977.

Bettis, Stan. *Market Days, An Informal History of the Eugene Producers' Public Market*. Eugene: Lane Pomona Grange Fraternal Society, 1969.

Bowen, William A. *The Willamette Valley: Migration and Settlement on the Oregon Frontier*. Seattle: University of Washington Press, 1978.

Buan, Carolyn M. and Lewis, Richard, Eds. *The First Oregonians, An Illustrated Collection of Essays on Traditional Lifeways, Federal-Indian Relations, and the State's Native People Today*. Portland: Oregon Council for the Humanities, 1991.

McArthur, Lewis L. *Oregon Geographic Names*. Portland, Oregon Historical Society, 1982.

Metzler, Ken, Ed. *Yesterday's Adventure: A Photographic History of Lane County, Oregon*. Eugene: Lane County Historical Society, 1998.

Moore, Lucia W.; McCornack, Nina W.; and McReady, Gladys W. *The Story of Eugene*. Lane County Historical Society, 1995.

Peterson, Pete. *Our Wagon Train Is Lost*. Eugene: New American Gothic, 1975.

Sekora, Lynda. *Springfield, Oregon Historical Context Statement*. Oregon City: Koler/Morrison Planning Consultants, 1991.

Velasco, Aldo, Ed. *The Millers, A History of Springfield High School*. Springfield: Springfield High School, 1988.

Velasco, Dorothy. *Lane County: An Illustrated History of the Emerald Empire*. Windsor Publications, 1985.

Walling, Albert G. *Illustrated History of Lane County, Oregon*. Portland: A.G. Walling, 1884.

Warner, Agnes Stewart. *Diary*. Transcribed and reproduced. Eugene: Lane County Historical Society, 1961.

Zucker, Jeff; Hummel, Kay; and Hogfoss, Bob. *Oregon Indians — Culture, History and Current Affairs*. Portland: Western Imprints (Oregon Historical Society) 1983.

NEWSPAPERS
The Register-Guard
The Springfield News

PERIODICALS
Lane County Historian
Springfield Museum: Brochures and unpublished materials

ACKNOWLEDGMENTS

The authors would like to express deepest gratitude to Kathy Jensen and Estelle McCafferty of the Springfield Museum. Their tireless and constantly cheerful participation was immeasurable. We are also grateful to Dan Egan, Marilyn Waff, and Denise Brittain, Springfield Area Chamber of Commerce; Tom Draggoo and the book committee; John Tamulonis and Joseph Leahy, City of Springfield; Dr. Thomas Connolly, Oregon State Museum of Anthropology; Patty Krier, University of Oregon Museum of Natural History; Jason Koski, Kim Sullivan, *The Springfield News*; Mary Ann Rhodes, Springfield Utility Board; Moderne Studio; Chris Pryor, Barbara Zentner, and Ken Long, Willamalane Park and Recreation District; KMTR; Monica Shovlin, Sony; Lisa Van Winkle, Weyerhaeuser; Gordon Culbertson, Rosboro Lumber; UO Athletic Department; Rob Romig, *The Register-Guard*; Ed Harms, Bill Morrisette, Leonard Clearwater, Don Lutes, Sue Kesey, Kathleen Caprario, Sparky J. Roberts, George & Cristy Beltran, Blake Hastings, Pat Albright, Al Brandt, Jack Criswell, Claude Gerlach, Don Ebbert, Lance Freeman, Bill Haggerty, Hugh Hassell, Bill Lewellen, George Litzenberger, Robert Moffitt, John McCulley, John Nelson, B.J. Rogers, Jerry Brown, Lee Dillon, Ed Bennett, George Morris, and Bill Mansell.

INDEX